DON'T KILL THE MESSENGER

A MOTORBIKE CRASH. A STORY OF RECOVERY.

DON'T KILL THE MESSENGER

A MOTORBIKE CRASH. A STORY OF RECOVERY.

K. L. Hill

This book is dedicated to Paul's family and the memory of Paul.

CONTENTS

CHAPTER 1

THE ACCIDENT

I was getting really fed up with them. For a few weeks, I had been having some weird dreams, each one a variation on the same theme. For instance, I would be celebrating my 32nd birthday, and everything would be going with a swing. Then, I would either fall out of a window of a high-rise building or be stabbed by a guest at a party, or I'd walk through the front door of my home and be hit by a passing car. All of the dreams, perhaps, I should say nightmares, had the same inevitable ending... death: *my* death, to be precise. I would awake with a jolt just at the point of my imminent demise, so I never experienced death itself but suffered the terrible feeling of it being the end for a split second. They were very odd dreams, which was strange considering the type of person I am.

I'm a down-to-earth sort of bloke—a family man—who, at that time, had a wife and three small children. I was working seven days a week for the National Coal Board as an electrician in the mine. My father before me had also worked at the pit; he was a mechanical engineer and a very good one, too. I lived in an area where the coal board, "the NCB", was the biggest employer. I worked that bloody hard, taking overtime regularly to bump up my wages, that by the time I went to bed in the evening, I was knackered and usually went 'out like a light' as soon as my head hit the pillow. I didn't have any problem sleeping. On the nights I wasn't working at the pit, I often did shifts at the local pubs and nightclubs as a bouncer on the doors to get the extra cash me and my family needed. I had to be up at 5 o'clock in the morning. I would make up and light the coal fire so that my wife, Gill and the three children would feel warm when they needed to start their day.

After experiencing the dreams a few times, I was getting a little disturbed by their consistency and told Gill and a couple of my friends about them. I felt a bit daft mentioning them, but I never dwelled on them for long. There were other pressing things I had to attend to. Everyday matters took up more of my thoughts, like ensuring I met the mortgage repayments, thinking how I could afford to give the kids a treat from time to time and also guaranteeing Gill was supported as much as I was able. The overtime was really handy as our finances were pushed to the limit.

Gill had initially spotted the bungalow where we had lived for a couple of years, and although priced higher than what we could comfortably afford, we decided to go for it. I was financially stretched to the maximum, but we liked it, and it had a lovely big garden for the kids to play in. So, I had no time for idle thoughts and dwelling on my dreams. I didn't consider them to have much significance, and it didn't even enter my head that they had any hidden meaning or could even be some kind of prophecy. All I wanted at the time was a good night's sleep and to keep working hard to bring in the money so my wife and kids could live as comfortable a life as I could manage for them. Life was hard at times, but good. We were happy, and what we were achieving as a family was down to good, honest graft and teamwork. Typical of a working-class family born in a mining village in the Midlands, I expect.

I have never believed in any paranormal type of mumbo jumbo. I still don't, if it comes to that, but what happened to me does make you think about it. Well, it more than makes you think. It turned my world and my family's world upside down, and it would never be the same again. Call it fate if you like. I am definitely a changed man through it. It shaped my future. It makes me what I am now. Fate...

We had attended the wedding of Ian and Emma, who were our best friends. It was a lovely May morning, and my two young, blonde, mop-haired daughters, Gemma and Rachel, had made adorable bridesmaids. Their flouncy white dresses decorated with tiny pink rosebuds were lovely. They had little pumps on their feet and carried small pom-pom balls of flowers. They really enjoyed being dressed up like princesses, and Chris, my little boy, made a very cute pageboy. All 'dressed up to the nines' too, Gill spent her time herding the giggling kids.

Emma looked stunning, like every bride should. She was a very pretty girl with a pale complexion and loads of light, tumbling blonde curls. She was dressed in a traditional wedding gown. Ian looked every inch the proud groom. He struck quite a handsome figure with his swarthy, dark looks. It was a lovely day, and we all enjoyed ourselves.

I had known Ian for a few years. He was a little younger than me, but we both shared the same passion... motorbikes. Our families had holidayed together the previous summer. Gill and Emma had taken the kids in the car to Newquay, and Ian and I had enjoyed the journey on our motorbikes. We had attended bike meets together and had enjoyed trips to Donington Park racetrack to watch the Motor GP. We had shared some good times. Although there were no discussions on bikes at the wedding, it was a topic of conversation at the evening reception, as invariably it was when we got our heads together over a pint.

Matt was Ian's younger brother and had been his best man. He was a little nervous at the earlier ceremony because he was only 18 years old and, therefore, found it a bit daunting. Everyone was relaxed, and the wine and beer were flowing in the evening. I told them I had put in for a day's leave from work for the following Monday, and I was telling them how much I was looking forward to test riding a motorbike from the local motorbike shop at Clay Cross, a nearby town. I was in possession of a beautiful red Kawasaki bike that Gill had put a down payment on the previous year. We couldn't really afford it at the time, but she felt I needed some kind of relief from the heavy workload that I was doing. I couldn't have been happier when I took the surprise delivery of it. However, it still didn't stop me from eyeing up the new models when they came into the shop. Although I had no intentions of buying, I was really going to enjoy the test ride on a newer version of a Kawasaki bike.

Matt had just started work at a supermarket in town as a trainee manager and had a little cash available. He couldn't wait to upgrade his motorbike to a larger one and follow in his brother's footsteps as a 'proper biker'. He asked if he could come along with me for a test ride session but pleaded with me to rearrange with the shop to make it a Wednesday, as that was when he could get the time off work. It would be a bit of a hassle for me, but he was so excited about it that I didn't want to let him down. So Wednesday it was. I knew he looked up to me and would be glad to have me available to pick my brains on the day on the various specifications and the pros and cons of the different models available.

Wednesday came. It was the 10th of May. The date would be etched indelibly in my memory forever more. I didn't know that, though, when I set off on the lovely sunny morning to pick up Matt. I went to his house just a couple of miles from where I lived. He was already eagerly awaiting my arrival. I could feel his excitement as he climbed onto the pillion seat behind me. We set off down the road, and I couldn't resist opening the throttle for a quick burst of acceleration. It was only for a couple of hundred yards, but wow! What a feeling! I didn't want to set a bad example, though, and after giving him a taste of what could be experienced on the lovely machines, I decided to settle down to show him how to ride carefully and safely. He was only 18, after all, and I remember myself being that age, knowing how impressionable you can be.

I had taken some silly chances in the past and didn't want to give him the wrong idea about biking. It is great fun, but you need to be responsible and alert, much more so than a car driver, and you need to respect the motorbike you are riding. In my youth, I had several near misses and a couple of "offs", mainly a result of my hot-headedness or not looking far enough ahead. For the rest of the journey, I planned to show him how a good rider should handle his bike.

I was nearing the bike shop and approaching the final roundabout. The national speed limit was signposted as the maximum speed for the road. But with the roundabout ahead and a petrol station on the left, I shut off the throttle and was going about 50 miles per hour. There was a milk float parked just before the petrol station entrance with its nearside wheels on the kerb. I clocked the situation and positioned myself more towards the centre of the road to give a wider berth to the parked float. I was about to pass it, and then, out of the blue, a car appeared in front of me. It had pulled out of the petrol station. I saw it for a split second. My reflexes kicked in, and I was able to veer just to the right. The slight adjustment I made resulted in me narrowly missing the driver's door, but did not give us enough time to manoeuvre to safety on the bike. However, I did enough to save the driver of the car from the full force of the impact.

We whacked into the wing with tremendous force. It was carnage. The lady driver escaped the crash unscathed. Matt and I, unfortunately, weren't so lucky. My pelvis ploughed into the petrol tank. My hands and wrists took some of the force of impact on the handlebars. My thumbs were forced backwards on the bars. I remember the pain so clearly; even today I do. I flew through the air before hitting the road quick and hard. My whole body was racked with pain on impact. As soon as I saw the car coming towards us, in that split second, I thought that was it. I was a goner. Everything I did was pure instinct. As I lay on the road, I couldn't understand why I wasn't dead. I was conscious; maybe I was about to die at any moment. I drifted in and out of consciousness, but I had an unusual calmness about me: an acceptance of the situation and what I thought was the inevitable. My arms were positioned on my pelvis, but my hands felt warm and wet, as did my groin and thighs. I felt mushy. I had hit the road with my right side. I knew my shoulder was all crunched. My head had also hit the tarmac heavily. It must have been the blood I could feel, but I couldn't understand what it was at the time. It just felt warm and pulpy. It just felt strange. I just lay there confused and helpless, wondering if I was just going to lose consciousness and maybe not wake up. The pain was immense.

I shut my eyes for a moment, and I opened them slowly. I was still amazed I could do so. A middle-aged man was leaning over me. It was a surreal moment. He wasn't a complete stranger, but a familiar face of a man. My vision was hazy, but I knew this was no heavenly body ready to lead me up to the pearly gates. I recognised the face straight away. I could see his concerned and worried face, but it gave me comfort. I knew this man, and I knew it was someone I could trust. His lips were moving; he was talking to me and reassuring me. The calmness of the voice put me more at ease. I knew him well. It was Maurice Feltham, my old metalwork teacher from school. He was also a keen motorbike enthusiast. He had gone on after leaving teaching to own a motorbike shop, and years later, Maurice and his sons actually owned the motorbike shop I had gone to visit. Coincidences in life, hey? He had been in the petrol station and heard the crash. I was so glad to see that familiar face; I was so glad I was still hanging on.

"Does it look bad, Maurice?" I said weakly.

"Just lie still, lad. I'm afraid it does. The ambulance men are here, and they'll sort you out."

Then, like a thunderbolt, a thought hit me. *God, Matt.*

"Maurice. How's my mate? Is he ok?"

"He's being seen to, lad. He's in good hands now," he said.

I was always thankful for how Maurice talked to me that day. I'm glad it was someone like him who I first saw when I opened my eyes. There would be no lies to mask the reality. There was a calmness to his voice and practical reactions to my questions. I could see the empathy on his face and the need to make me feel better, which he did.

The next person I saw was a policeman looking into my face and saying, "What's happened here, then?"

I was struggling to think about the question. "I don't know what happened. The car just pulled out." My memory was fuzzy in parts, but no wonder, as my life's blood was still draining out of me.

I must then have lost consciousness for a little while. I was told later that efforts were made to take off my helmet, but I remembered, even in the bad state I was in, that they shouldn't do that. Awful stories of what can happen when helmets are taken off without stabilising the neck were conscious thoughts in my head, albeit intermittently. I had heard various stories, such as the one of a man whose helmet had been taken off at the scene of an accident and part of the skull had been removed with it. Apparently, I protested very loudly to keep the helmet on, and it was upsetting and frustrating to know that although I was protesting strongly about the removal of my helmet, it was taken off my head anyway. Things did get a little muddled at about this time. I eventually lost consciousness totally as I was getting weaker. I don't remember much about anything after that for quite a while. I do remember the police bending over me, asking me questions. I wasn't fully lucid, but I do recall answering and telling the police that the car came from nowhere.

When I opened my eyes again, I was in the back of the ambulance, but I had no recollection of how I got in there.

The driver was on the radio. "Bringing the second one in now. Expected DOA."

My initial feeling right then was *Oh, my God.* I was going to die.

In fact, I did die... twice. The defibrillators were brought into action both times, and I was jump-started back to life. I can't remember the end of the journey to hospital, or anything for three weeks after that. I lay in a coma, knowing nothing at all. Family members came and went, except for the kids. It was considered they were too young to deal with how I looked, and it would cause them trauma. I was oblivious to any activity happening around me. I was unaware of the impact the accident had brought on my family, Matt's family, and all the other lives that it had affected in one way or another.

When I did awake, I was frightened and scared. I didn't know where I was, and I couldn't move or talk. I had pipes sewn into my neck and a big fat tube down my throat. I didn't want it in there, but I couldn't move my hands to take it out. I was oh so thirsty. I was totally parched, but helpless to do anything at all. I didn't know where the hell I was. I wanted to scream. I wanted someone to answer my questions, which I couldn't ask out loud because of the great big fat pipe. My eyes were operating ok, and my eyeballs must have been swivelling in their sockets with fear and anxiousness. All I could do was see and roll my eyeballs around, but I couldn't move the rest of my body. I couldn't communicate anything to anyone except with my eyes, but there was no one there. I felt trapped. Machines surrounded me and were bleeping away. People peered at me, but then disappeared.

A few days passed like this. I was in my own isolated world, and I felt like a circus freak in a peep show. I was looked at, and the monitors at the side of my bed were checked frequently. Faces appeared, and I tried to focus, but then they'd disappear. I would then be left alone with just the sound of the bleeps from the machine, an endless monotone. The pipe in my throat made me gag. I wanted to shout. I wanted them to hear me. *I am here. Will someone take this fucking pipe out of my mouth?* I could only think it, which added to the fear and frustration I was feeling. Why wasn't anyone communicating with me? *Hello. Somebody? Anybody? I am here, behind these eyes, and I need help.*

The pain hadn't kicked in at that stage, as I had been heavily drugged with morphine to relieve the agony. However, I had overwhelming feelings of wretchedness, helplessness, and complete and utter emotions of frustration and isolation. I was so thirsty... so fucking thirsty. I drifted in and out of consciousness in a twilight, hazy world. I vaguely remember the images peering over me. My wife, my mother, my older sister and even my dad. *Dad, God! What a turn-up for the books! It must be serious for him to come.*

Apparently, at one stage, the doctors thought that my right arm was too damaged to save. They had asked Gill's permission to amputate, but she refused.

"Oh no," she said. "He'd kill me when he wakes up if you do that."

If there is one thing I am always indebted to her for, it was for that decision she made to say no.

A couple of weeks later, POW! The pain kicked in. God! Did it kick in? I can't say there was a single part of my body that hurt more than another. I was just one mass of racked pain. I thought I couldn't bear it. I couldn't roll over or move to alter the pattern of the pain. Tears would roll down my face. I had to bear it, and I did, of course. There was no other choice, but I really don't know how I got through it. I became more aware of my surroundings and myself as the doctors started to cut down the amount of drugs I was being administered. I preferred the drug-induced world—the one where I was free of pain and misery. More and more cold reality was released upon me every day as the morphine was reduced. There was a non-stop rally of nurses checking, measuring and adjusting all the various pipes and monitors that were inserted or attached all over my body.

It was during one of these checks that the sheet was lifted and I was able to peer downwards. I had been aware that my legs were spread-eagled on the bed, and when I looked, I could see why. There appeared to be a football placed between my thighs. When my eyes had focused more clearly, I could see the football wasn't a football after all, but my ball, my left ball, to be precise. It was the only testicle remaining, a very bright purple colour, and it would have been more fitting on a baboon. With the tubes sewn in my neck and inserted down my throat, I felt like a part of a big sci-fi machine in a film—just a brain being kept alive. The body wasn't mine to control.

But the pain! God, I just couldn't stand it! With a huge effort, I lifted both my arms, which were heavily strapped with splints and bandages. I couldn't bend my arms, but I managed to grab either side of the pipe and yank it up my throat and out of my mouth. My breathing altered immediately. It took a while to realise where the sound of the short, shallow pants was coming from. The quick gasps of air were erratic. I sounded like a pair of small bellows working on overdrive. The nurse lunged forward to try to stop me, but she wasn't quick enough.

I drifted off again only to find that when I woke, the pipe hadn't been replaced. I was breathing, albeit with difficulty, on my own. My throat was dry, oh, so dry, and it felt so much better without the pipe. The pain was overpowering, but at last, I could do something and was able to take back a little control over my own body. Not much! But I shouted for all my worth in frustration. God knows where I got the strength, but I shouted as loud as I was able.

"Someone shoot me! For God's sake, fucking shoot me. I can't fucking stand it anymore. Shoot me now!" I demanded it; I was ordering it, but I was ignored. I don't usually swear, but I felt it was needed to show how much I wanted the staff to take action.

The staff flittered past, not even looking my way, afraid of any eye contact with me. They pretended it wasn't happening. The young nurses didn't know how to deal with me. I shouted and shouted over and over again. I cursed them all, and tears rolled down my face. I was exhausted, but still I shouted, and when that approach appeared to be futile, I pleaded.

"Please get me a gun. Please... please get me a gun. I'll do it. I'll do it. I'll pull the trigger myself somehow."

Then I begged; begged anyone and everyone for release, even God. Then came hopelessness. I was broken. I was still shouting and pleading pitifully. I can't remember what I was saying in the end, but I was crying like a baby. One of the nurses got a doctor to my bed. He explained that I had received the full amount of morphine they felt was safe to give and all the pain relief they could offer, and they had to let my body rest from it. There was only one drug left to administer as a last resort. It would knock me out, but it was a hallucinogenic drug, and it would give me bad nightmares. I could only have one dose. I didn't even have to think about it.

"Just give it to me," I begged.

They administered the injection, and I drifted into sleep. At least that's what they called it, but what a nightmare, and it seemed to last hours and hours. Monsters, giant spiders, strange worlds, cliffs to fall off, and aliens chasing me. The physical pain was gone, but I seemed to spend endless hours scared shitless in the world of devils and demons. While my body rested, my brain was as active as a full-on steam locomotive on a journey through hell.

I was oblivious to the worry and concern of the doctors who were daily trying to save my life. My pelvis was shattered and was proving a big problem for the doctors as they tried to think of ideas to stabilise it. They needed to strengthen it somehow. My legs were a mess, although not a priority for the surgeons, as leg injury is not life-threatening. My back was broken in three places, but thankfully, my spinal cord was intact. I learnt later that they had asked the surgeon who had helped fix Barry Sheene's bones after his big motorcycle Grand Prix accident to work on me, but he wasn't available at that particular time, and the doctors needed to act quickly. Thanks to the innovative idea of a young surgeon named Mr Scott, an operation was done on my pelvis. It involved threading the bones together with a steel line. The idea was to take the steel wire out when it had done its job: when my pelvis had stabilised.

After one of the operations, I came around and found myself looking in the face of a young surgeon. Doctor Lawrence Coldicote had been operating on me in the theatre and was slumped in a chair in my room. He was asleep and looked tired out. Apparently, he'd been working many hours on me and yet didn't go home at the end of his shift. He chose to stay throughout the night with me until I came around from the surgery to ensure he was available if an emergency occurred. The doctors and medical staff showed such dedication, for which I will be eternally grateful. Without their innovative ideas on how to put me back together and their care and selfless dedication, I would not be here today and certainly not in the condition I am in now.

For all that people sometimes say about the National Health Service, I can't fault 'em. In the first weeks after the accident, I had eight life-saving operations and a total of 89 pints of blood and plasma. It was some type of record at the time, but it wasn't really the way I wanted to achieve a claim to fame. One of the consultants told me that if a patient gets to where they have had 50 pints of blood, the chances of them living were very slim. I was told later that the operating theatre was filled with every expert: specialised surgeons and doctors in their field. Fate must have had a part to play. I'd lost such a vast amount of blood I should have been dead, but the blood that remained in my body was in all the important areas. I'm not sure to this day what organs were removed. I'm not even sure if I have my spleen or appendix.

Visitors came and went. My dad still visited, too, and I know he felt awkward. He didn't have very much to say when he came, but then again, he didn't say much to me at the best of times, anyway. He did his dutiful visit, but I could sometimes see the concern etched on his face. He no doubt thought his usual of me. I was used to him calling me a "big, daft bugger". However, I knew even he was worried about my wellbeing.

He was, in the main, a grumpy old man, not like me at all. I had at least inherited my love of bikes and mechanical engines from him. He had been an army sergeant in the REME in the Second World War and had been a despatch rider in Europe on his motorbike. He regularly had some kind of engine stripped down in the kitchen, and the only time he seemed to interact with me was when either my friends or I asked him for help on our bikes or cars. He would then participate with enthusiasm and discuss ideas with us. He was one of the few mechanics I knew who had the special ability to diagnose what was wrong with an engine by touching a screwdriver to it whilst it was running. He put the handle end to his ear, and from listening to the engine noise, he could then deduce where the problem was; an amazing talent.

Neither of us would admit it, but we had more in common than we gave each other credit for. I wish I could tell him that now, but sadly, I can't. He looked after his money carefully, let's say. He was tight with his money and even tighter with his affection. He's passed on now. It makes me smile as I get older; the amount of people in the village who tell me how much I look like my dad. I have to accept, therefore, that I do. I kid people that the only things I inherited from my dad were a big nose and a bald head, but as I have got older, I now know better. I respect the talent he had with the engines. I wish I could share our time working together on something we both loved and had in common.

He did look the concerned father when he visited me in the hospital; therefore, I know I must have looked in a bad way. He didn't part with his sympathy too easily and was thoroughly embarrassed by any show of emotion. He was a product of his times, I suppose. It wasn't manly to be emotional. He was a strong disciplinarian, and I had often felt the whack of his leather belt on my behind many times. I was also sent to bed with no supper on numerous occasions. Mum used to sneak some food up for me, though, usually a nice sandwich. He was over 40 before I was born.

A few years after his death, my mother passed on to me his handwritten notebooks, which contain beautifully drawn detailed diagrams of engines. I also received some of his tools that he had accumulated over his working years as a fitter. Unfortunately, they were to be stolen from my garage at a later date. The tools were probably of no intrinsic value to the thief, but I lost a wealth of sentimental value. A hard man though my dad was, I think of him now with some love and warmth and more understanding of why he was the way he was. He was a product of the times he was brought up in. I should have told him I loved him at the time, but I don't think he would have appreciated it. He probably would have just said, "You big, daft bugger."

Gill came to see me every day, which was a task in itself when you think she had the kids to sort out and look after. My auntie would take care of the kids whilst Gill came to the hospital. Auntie Lillian was my mum's sister. She had no children of her own but rallied round with other relatives to make sure the babysitting was covered. She used to take the kids on day trips and the like so that they could enjoy summer days like all other children at the time. Letting them behave like children, having fun. Bless you, Auntie Lilly.

At times, I feel a little bad at the fun we used to poke at her. She was small and wore thick-lensed glasses. My cousin and I would squash in our faces with our hands and say, "Googie, googie" behind her back when we were little, I'm ashamed to say. I don't know why we did it. I don't even know what "googie" means, but my cousin and I would roll about on the floor saying "Googie, googie" until tears rolled down our faces. Auntie Lillian would get mad at us and say she would tell our mothers that we'd been monkeys, and she used to slap our legs. When it is needed, though, families do rally together. Mining villages usually had extended families to call upon, and Staveley was no different. Aunties, cousins and grandmas either lived on the same street or in the streets close by. Extended family members are invaluable at a time like this.

The long-term prognosis of my physical condition didn't worry me at that time; I was too busy trying to get through each day. It was the least of my problems. My state of consciousness still varied from day to day. At night, the pain was so bad I thought I couldn't bear to get through it. In a semi-conscious condition, I decided that was it. I'd done with life. I wanted to fall asleep and slip into oblivion, but I had no choice. Each night came and went, and every day, I woke up, still hanging in there. Although I was rushed down to the operating theatre on numerous occasions to overcome some kind of life-threatening battle on the operating table, after each operation, my body managed to pull through. The doctors said I survived mainly because of the excellent physical condition my body was in before the accident. They said I should have been thankful. I didn't appreciate them saying so, and thanking them for saving my life was the last thought on my mind back then.

As well as my "wonderful" physique, stubbornness, willpower and bloody-mindedness were attributes which helped me get through, too. I was in quite good shape as

I'd trained at the gym for years, was quite proficient at karate, and had kept up the strength and fitness exercises. I used to run miles in bare feet and was really disciplined in the training I did. In the big general miner's strike that had hit the country a few years before, I had taken the opportunity to use the time to do hours at the gym, and I was still in the habit of training most days. I had been as 'fit as a fiddle'. My days as a bouncer on the doors of nightclubs had given me a bit of a reputation. There was always someone who would want to 'have a go'. I wasn't the trouble-causing type, but I could handle myself if it came along, and I never backed off even when tackling knife and axe-wielding nutters. Staveley is, after all, a hard and gritty Derbyshire town. I had a few mishaps on the way, even losing some teeth once, but it was all part of the life in the community where I lived. If anyone wanted trouble (usually when fuelled by drink), they could "Bring it on." When I thought of such brawly Saturday nights as I lay in my hospital bed, I couldn't help welling up. It was a far cry from the wreck of the man I had become. There was nothing I could do. No one to fight to make it right. The only battle I could offer now was with my own body to hang on physically and to care about hanging on emotionally. I lay there like a baby, useless, and with all my needs depending on the assistance of others. I remember being exhausted and crying like a baby, too. Where was that strong man? Maybe he'd never return. Somewhere deep, deep inside of me, a tiny little bit of my former self must have been lurking, but I wasn't aware of it then.

CHAPTER 2

THE AWAKENING

Emma came to see me in those early weeks, and the first time I recognised her, it really cheered me. By this stage, I could move my arms a little, even though they were wrapped and bandaged down to my fingertips. Still, I was able to tease her and tried to cross my hands to form a cross as if warding off evil spirits. She had seen me do this many times before, but it had never brought tears to her eyes like that time. She told me later how frail and tired I'd looked, and yet I still tried to get her to smile. She found it too much and left in tears.

The police had managed to inform Ian and Emma of the accident as they were about to start their honeymoon. They were at the airport, but obviously didn't take the scheduled flight after they had heard the devastating news of what had happened.

I had been asking about Matt, but I never got any straight answers. With the influence of the drugs diminishing each day, my mind started to work more and more logically. I knew the accident was a bad one and that I was in the intensive care unit, but Matt wasn't with me. If he had been in a normal surgical ward, he would have come to see me. So where was he, and why would no one answer me properly when I asked them?

Before Ian started to tell me the truth, I knew in my heart of hearts what the answer to my question was, but when the words left his mouth, I wanted to crumble up and tear out my heart. It was truly unbearable. That night, when the pain racked through my body, my thoughts were different. The pain was the least I deserved. I had lived, and Matt had died, and the pain and grief were too much. How could I carry on living knowing that? I didn't want the physical pain anymore, and I couldn't stand the mental pain. I bellowed and cried throughout the night.

"Oh, God! Oh, God. Why didn't I die too? It wasn't fair. Who decided that he would have to go and I would be left behind? He was only 18, for God's sake. I didn't deserve to be still alive. Why can't I just fall asleep and not wake up? His poor family. How could I face them? Why couldn't I have looked after him? Why did I say yes? Why did I agree to change the day, the time? Why didn't I just say no, that he couldn't come?"

Of course, everyone on the ward tried to block out my shouts. They could hear me but were embarrassed by my outburst. No one could bear to listen. Not the patients or the staff on the patients in the ward. The emotional display made them feel uncomfortable, and they didn't know how to cope with it. How could anyone know how it all felt?

No one could help me. There were only Matt and me on that bike: two people together, sharing what turned out to be his last moments. Matt was gone. I was left behind in this world, but my life would be changed forever. I was so... so alone, and I should have been with Matt. God should have been kinder, and if it was his turn to go, he should have taken us both or left us both alone. I was there to escort him that day and to protect him. I should have gone with him on his final journey. As a friend of his big brother, I had a role to play. Yet I didn't keep him safe, and I should have left this world with him.

What the hell was God doing? He wasn't playing fair. Every morning I awoke after that day was another hard day to get through. I didn't think my mind or body could take any more, but I managed some kind of sleep each day and awoke every morning. Unfortunately, I had not died. I so much wished for that peace, but I had to find a way to accept I was still in this world and discover a way to live with the pain and guilt and go on.

For 13 weeks, I had to lie totally immobilised on my back whilst my pelvis knitted back together. It felt like an eternity, but I mended well. The only thing I could do all that time was to think and think and rethink my past and my future. I did a hell of a lot of thinking, and sometimes it made my brain hurt. I couldn't stop it. It did sink in that I was going to survive now, and I had to sort my head out as to what direction I was going to take. My wife and my kids would get the benefit of a better husband and a better dad. I wanted to be a better person for everyone. One thing was for sure: I needed to reinvent myself. I wasn't able to be the same person. I would get stronger, go back to work, be less angry and have more patience. I would pay back my family for all the trouble I had been.

I grew accustomed to the tediousness of my physical situation. I learnt to take one day at a time. I had no choice. I planned, I reasoned, and I mentally grew stronger. I stopped crying every day. I needed to move on. Sometimes, unexpectedly, the darker thoughts caught me off guard. A great sadness about Matt and tremendous guilt would cloud over me, and I would sink into the abyss. I had to force myself back on track.

Concentrating on my master plan brought me back into the light—the plan of getting myself back into life. I didn't dare dwell on Matt and my health for very long as I would start to sink so very quickly and lose control. I learnt how to take stock and cope. I had to, and eventually, it started to work. Some days were actually bearable. Some days, I didn't want to die; I wanted to live. I wanted to get better, and I wanted to go home to my family, to look after them and to resume my role. By keeping my thoughts on my plan, I could stop myself from descending into depression, and I had some control over something: my mind, and ultimately, my wellbeing.

After the 13 weeks, I was aided to sit up. It was like I was drunk on a ship in rough seas. I got seasick, and I wasn't even out of bed. The room spun around, and I had to throw up. After I managed a couple of minutes, I had to rest back down, and then I'd try again for a little longer. Eventually, I could sit up for a few minutes. It was about this time I was paid a visit by the police. They wanted to ask me a few questions about the accident and had been waiting for my health to improve and for permission from the doctor, but they didn't waste any time. I was placed in a wheelchair, which had been heavily padded out to ease the pressure on my broken bones. Just sitting in the chair was a challenge in itself. I felt ill from the moment they started. I still felt very delicate sitting up, but the two policemen showed no mercy. I was bombarded with question after question.

"How many feet per second would you be travelling at 80 miles per hour?"

They smirked at me, then at each other.

How the fuck do I know? I thought. I was feeling sick and wanted this interview over.

"So you don't know then?" and again, "So! You don't know," they jibed.

It was more of a statement than a question.

I had learnt to ride a bike before I learnt to drive a car. I'd had my licence since I was 17 years old, but I was still sharp and very experienced. I kept my bike in the best of condition and took pride in doing so, a trait I had inherited from my dad. I always checked my lights and indicators before setting off. I'd travelled that road many times. The motorbike shop was a favourite haunt of a lot of local bikers. I didn't do anything wrong that day, and yet they were making me feel like a criminal. I asked them a question.

"How many feet per second would *you* be travelling if you were going 60 miles an hour?"

They looked at each other and one stammered, "Err, well. Well... I'm not sure."

I rest my fucking case. Who the hell did they think they were? They weren't interested in the facts. I was a motorbike rider and, therefore, guilty by default.

Why didn't they go and ask the stupid woman who pulled out blindly in front of my bike while I was going no more than 50 miles an hour? I started to feel nauseous from being in the chair for too long. I had been interrogated for about an hour, and I was feeling rough. I needed to get back into bed. They left, and I was feeling pretty gutted. It hadn't occurred to me before then that people would actually think it was my fault and that I was speeding. My God! It was bad enough living with the guilt without having official speculation over who was responsible for the crash. I had been instructed to get a solicitor to represent me and chose one from the local practice in the village. I soon realised how much I would need one. The actual legal processes were very slow, and little did I know at the time that this was the beginning of a long and emotionally draining battle.

Gill, I learnt later, had kept the headline of the local paper from me: "High-Speed Crash Ends in Death". Once I eventually read the headline myself, it would be years until I ever bought another local newspaper, in fact, any kind of newspaper. I wanted to drag the editor over the top of his large and highly polished desk and give him a good slap. The journalist had quoted a witness (an old lady walking up the pavement of the road where the accident occurred). Apparently, the witness had said that a motorbike had passed her at high speed. I myself had passed a few bikes on that road because the venue we were going to was a popular place with bikers. There were always numerous bikes on that road throughout the summer months. She didn't know one bike from another, and let's face it, to someone in their dotage, anything travelling at 40 miles an hour would seem to be travelling fast. However, because the paper had quoted a so-called witness, they were in their power to take the opinion of the "witness" and use the statement to form the basis of their article and use the quote as a headline. It still peeves me even today, the power the press has. To be able to manipulate statements for the sake of sensationalism whilst still staying within the limits of the law is truly sickening.

Gill continued to visit me every day, but it was a while before she brought the children. My mum and auntie carried on with a rota system to help with looking after the children, even having them overnight so that Gill could devote time to me at the hospital. I needed her there with me. I depended on her support like a crutch. Managing without her didn't bear thinking about.

I asked the doctors about my health continuously.

"When will I walk again? When will I be able to go home?"

All they had were flaky answers. They just told me to take one day at a time and be patient. The answers were of no use to me at all. I needed to have definite answers, not the hairy fairy ones I was getting. They didn't know what the prognosis was. They told me to expect the worst and maybe to get my head around the fact I probably wouldn't walk again. Just in case that became the reality. I couldn't live like that. I needed more than hope against all odds. I wanted a guarantee from them that it would all be fine, even if it was going to take time. I wasn't going to take 'maybe' as my approach to life in the future. If I was going to live and carry on with this life that I wasn't too bothered about staying in anyway, then it would be as a walking, talking, fully working, mobile man. I wasn't going to settle for anything less.

There was no doubt about the dedication and care I received from the doctors and nursing staff, but the list of damage to my body was a very extensive one. The pioneering operation to support my bones with the threaded steel wire had never been done before, but my pelvis was so delicate it needed to be held in place whilst the bone healed. They weren't sure if it would even work, but it meant me having to be immobilised for months after the operation in order for me to knit together properly. The huge catalogue of injuries meant not only had I become the first receiver of the pioneering "Scott wire", but there was also a long list of other injuries to be contended with. I'd suffered a bruised skull and brain as a result of my head hitting the road. It was very fortunate, however, that I had on a good-fitting helmet. Landing on my side had crunched my shoulder up to my neck, shattering my shoulder and some other bones. My thumbs had been broken backwards and were left dangling loosely in the skin. Both wrists were shattered, and the fingers on my right hand had twisted, rotated and broken. Most of my ribs were broken and had punctured my lung. My back was broken in three places. My pelvis, what was left of it, was shot forward and was sticking through my lower abdomen. I'd lost one testicle, and the other had to be partly removed afterwards, not to mention stitches in a rather delicate part of my anatomy. My legs were broken in various places. I had horrific internal injuries, and to this day, I don't know which organs they had to remove. I should not have been alive by all accounts. I have a lot to thank the hospital staff for, and I know that now, but at the time, as far as I was concerned, my life was over. I didn't deserve to be alive, but as I was then, I had to find a different way to live. As I was not worthy enough to be here for myself, I would proceed with my master plan: to provide a better life for my wife and children, who were struggling with the situation they had been left in because of what happened on that terrible day in May.

At that time, Gill was heaven sent. She was juggling the finances, looking after our children, visiting the hospital and was run off her feet. Everyone helped somehow. My cousin Paul, my often partner in crime since childhood, was cutting the lawn and doing the maintenance on our car. My work colleagues were calling in on Gill and offering their help where they could. Aid was coming in from various sources, and I was thankful for everyone being so supportive. Gill tried hard to keep the information for the children simple. They were very young and did not understand the situation fully, thank God! They knew their dad was poorly and in hospital and could not come home. The worries of finances were a real burden for Gill. She had given up her job in order to cope with the demands of the situation. My wages were paid for a while, but then they stopped. Then began the endless battle of form filling and phone calls to social services to apply for benefits. The mortgage repayments could not be met, and she found it all, understandably, a terrible strain.

The weeks turned into months, and I continued to lie there, immobile from the chest down. Although the doctors and consultants still could not give a definite prognosis on my condition, they doubted I would walk again. I never believed that for one moment, and I knew I would walk. The alternative was not an option. I stopped asking them after a while. Their answers frustrated me, and I knew better than them about how things were going to turn out. I was not contemplating any other option except a full recovery, no matter how long it took.

Going home was my main short-term aim, but that wish was quite a way from being granted, although I didn't know it at the time. I was determined to get better, however, and I was going to give my wife and children all the love and support I could give them as soon as I was able. I didn't let the doctor's opinion deter me. As I lay there hour after hour, day after day, the priorities in life became crystal clear. All the hours of thinking and pondering made everything appear so very black and white. Emotions would bubble up inside me and I would cry. This would happen often. What a turn-up for the books. I was so mad at myself. Me, Dan Church, behaving like a real wus.

What was wrong with my brain? It was so *not* like me. I didn't even feel like the same person in my head. My soul was in a black, black hole some days, and yet my body carried on, regardless. My thoughts sometimes seemed to be detached from my body, almost like two separate entities. Me – the man who had stood on the miners' picket line a few years earlier, defying anyone to cross, with my well-built frame forming part of the wall of miners, barring the way of any scabs who dared venture across the barrier of arm-linked men. Was I that same man? For years, it had become a way of life to weight-train until my muscles were well-honed and strong. Fearing no one and not averse to 'clocking' any chap who dared to sneer sideways in my direction. Was I still that man? No! There wasn't even a close resemblance mentally or physically to that man who had set off on his motorbike with his young friend on the sunny, bright morning of the 10th of May.

Even though months had passed, I still had some tubes and wires attached to me. A catheter had been fitted as my bladder had been badly torn, and the pain was excruciating every time a nurse replaced it. I also had a colostomy fitted. Needless to say, there was a huge hole in the vicinity of my bowels and intestines, but the doctors had juggled all the yards of sausage links of intestines and managed to get most of it back inside my stomach. I had wads of packing shoved into the gaping hole. This had to be changed often because of the risk of infection. Some of the flesh around the wound became very smelly and mangy-looking and had to be lopped off. It was dead flesh, and I didn't feel a thing except when the scissors trimmed the edge of healthy tissue, but the hole in my stomach looked even bigger. I was the human polo. I had a long steel rod through my knee to keep the kneecap in the right place. The ends stuck out on either side. There were small pins through my wrists, and the "Scott wire" was still in place in my pelvis. There were plans to remove it as soon as my pelvis had become strong enough. However, as my bones were mending at a tremendous rate, there had been calcification around the wire, and it was decided to leave it well alone.

When I was admitted to hospital, I had been a healthy 14 stone, 12 pounds in weight. I dropped to seven stone, and as I am six feet tall, I was one frail-looking man. I always had better self-esteem and more confidence in myself when I had trained because I felt my body made up for the fact that I had not been granted the looks of Adonis. *Far from it,* I thought. It didn't seem to detract the ladies, however. Maybe it was my natural charm and charisma. Who knows? As I said, my dad had never given me much in life but his bald head and large, sharp nose. My friends used to say that my face "showed character", which I think was the polite way of saying I wasn't a Brad Pitt type.

Thank heavens, then, for my strength of character or pig-headedness, whichever you may wish to call it. Whatever I lacked in natural physical attributes, I made up for in sheer bloody willpower and determination to make the most of what I had been given. Integrity, determination and, just as importantly, a good sense of humour can carry you a very long way.

There were some days when depression would take a hold of me. I would feel sorry for myself and feel myself start to crumble, and that was selfish. How could I, a man who should not have been alive, feel sorry for himself? I didn't matter anymore, and my whole purpose in life would be to add to other people's quality of life, people who were more worthy than I and deserved to be happy. This new objective of mine, in an odd way, helped me to rise above the depression. I didn't allow it to take root. On my good days, I started to joke and laugh with the nurses, and on my bad days, when the pains were bad, I tried not to be demanding – anything to make their days easier. I pretended to be someone else, and it worked. It was getting me through, and the days passed.

Most of the nurses were little gems and went out of their way for me. I was a 5-star guest. They kept Guinness in their fridges for me; apparently, it contains iron and is good for you. They would pick up a McDonald's burger on their way in for their shift. I'm not sure what medicinal benefit there is in a Big Mac, but it helped emotionally. I even had bacon butties for breakfast, much to the disdain of my fellow holiday campers who had to settle for cornflakes, and they weren't even Kellogg's. Some super saver crap, no doubt. After a while, it was not an effort to laugh and joke along with everyone. I was beginning to believe my own hype for happiness. It felt good. More and more often, I could feel a little glow of happiness spread within me. Perhaps not exactly happiness, but it wasn't sadness, and it felt good. For certain moments in time, I was happy I was alive. Sometimes, these moments were tinged with guilt for forgetting my purpose, but on the whole, life was getting easier.

Sometimes, I would have a bad night, and I would sink low. Matt would shoot to the forefront of my thoughts. Feelings of blackness, desolation and depression would begin to set in, and thoughts of longing to join him would enter my head. During these black times, I did not share my feelings with anyone, but maybe they knew. There were times when the staff gave me space and seemed to know I needed to be left alone. I never again bellowed out loudly. I learnt that nobody would understand and there was no point in trying to share my feelings. Nobody knew how I felt. They would be very lonely times. I would lie on my back, my head on the pillow, and cry silently, the tears trickling down my cheeks. Sometimes, I could propel myself forward out of the blackness by thinking, *Tomorrow is another day, and I will be stronger.*

The days followed in pretty much the same vein, some good and some bad. Patients in the ward came and went, and some good friendships were forged along the way. The bonds were sometimes very strong and similar to the ones struck up with my mining workmates: a camaraderie of people who share parts of their life at the most turbulent times.

There was one such friendship that I treasured the most during my time on the ward, and that was the friendship of an old man called John. He was a lovely man of 96 who had been living alone, independently, up to falling over and breaking his hip. He told lovely stories, and my life was enriched through knowing him. He was a true royalist and was really looking forward to receiving a telegram from the Queen for his 100th birthday. He was about to have a birthday and would be celebrating it in hospital because of his accident. I had asked the nurses to give the catering staff a message to make John a cake for his birthday, but the nurses came back and said the catering staff could not do it. I took this to heart, and I was livid. Was it too much to ask for one little bloody cake and a candle? I was so upset by the kitchen's response that when the menu preference form was delivered to me to select my choice for lunch for the following day, I told the kitchen staff exactly what I felt about them. I wrote a brief message at the bottom of the form for them. "Bloody mean bastards."

I was slightly worried afterwards because the jelly I received the following day tasted a bit odd, but as I didn't know what paraquat tasted like, I decided to eat it anyway. I was none the worse for it, so it seemed they had not taken offence over my little outburst. Perhaps they just did not care enough about anything. The cake would have been nice for John, though. It was a shame.

My children had started to visit me, which was great. Their visits reiterated my feeling that if I didn't feel worthy of living for myself, I could live to make the lives better for my children. They had gone through so much. My girls were bubbly and chatty, full of stories about school and friends. Chris, my little boy, was a unique little chap. He was very small for his age, even for a 5-year-old. He was quieter and more reserved than the girls. On one occasion, he had decided he did not want to leave the matchbox cars behind when he visited me, so he brought them along with him. Three down each sock. Some up his jumper and the rest under his woolly hat. They were only discovered when Gill made him remove his hat and an ambulance fell off his head. Followed by a dumper truck and a petrol tanker. As she peeled off his other layers of clothing, the whole collection came tumbling out. My little son had the entire ward in tears of laughter. The moment was made even funnier because he did not know what everyone found so funny.

All my children were favourites of John, and he used to call them over and push toffees into their little chubby hands. This made John a favourite of theirs. I used to chat with John, and he had some wonderful recollections of his life as a worker at Bolsover Castle National Trust building, where he staffed the entrance and handed out tickets. He told how he used to fetch up the water for the castle. I used to make him laugh with my gentle teasing. He always called the radio "the wireless", and he thought the television was still a new invention. When he didn't see me around, he would ask the nurses where I was, as I sometimes had to go for operations or scans. He said I cheered him up.

One night, coughing broke out on the ward, and the bouts of coughing were getting louder and longer. It was John. Earlier that day, I had gone to theatre for one of the many operations and obviously came back on the ward in a weakened, sleepy state. I tried to call out to John, but my voice was too quiet for anyone to hear, including John, and I wanted to give him some words of comfort and ask him if he was ok. In the end, I pressed my emergency buzzer to get the attention of the night nurse. She came scurrying in and I asked her to check on John. She drew the screen around his bed.

Throughout the night, John coughed and spluttered, and nurses ran in and out to attend to him. He got progressively worse. I knew he was bad because I had seen him before the screens were placed around him. I saw the colour drain from his face as if life itself was ebbing away from him. The nurses summoned a doctor. By the time the doctor had arrived, John had, unfortunately, already passed away. The nurses told me the news. I was gutted; really, really gutted. John's body was taken out in a metal box.

The next morning, his bed was stripped, and his "Get well" cards had gone. There was nothing left to show who had been in the bed only hours before. All signs of John had been eradicated from the ward and from my world. The space he left behind was so cold and empty. His death hit me very hard. I missed my friend very much and true to my form at the time, I cried. The ward was a lonelier place without him. A little ray of sunshine had gone. I think of him often and wish that he had managed to reach the age of 100 so that he would have been able to have the telegram he was so looking forward to receiving. It would have meant the world to him.

CHAPTER 3

ANGELS OF MERCY

Even today, anyone mentioning the word physiotherapy in earshot could get more than they bargained for, like me knocking their head off their shoulders. It conjures up such powerful emotions within me. There are flashbacks of pain and dread with visions of the therapists heading down the ward towards me. I had it explained to me by the doctors how essential it was to have the therapy, but the manipulations would bring on such intense pain that tears would roll down my cheeks. I did strike up somewhat of a love-hate relationship with the therapists, though, and it's probably best to think of the lighter side of those times.

There was one lady therapist who had really got me summed up. It was time for one of my "sessions", and she had already worked on some poor victims in my ward and was getting closer and closer to my bed. With each patient she tortured and left, I had an impending feeling of doom. It was soon to be my turn, but I wasn't having any of it. I had a cunning plan. I gently shut my eyes, deepened my breathing and lay there, trying to look as pathetic as I could. It worked. I could hear her footsteps getting more distant as she spoke.

"It looks like Mr Church has dropped off. I'd better leave him for today."

Good! Result! Or so I thought. I lay there for a minute or so more, just to be on the safe side, and slowly began to open my eyes. What a shock! Wide-opened blue eyes were inches away from my face.

"Hello, Mr Church," she said. "Glad to see you back with us after your little nap. You're just in time."

The smugness I had been feeling quickly disappeared. She had craftily tiptoed back up the ward just so that I wouldn't miss out on the valuable physio she was about to give me, and all free on the NHS, too. Such luck!

However, I can't help feeling that being a physiotherapist does have its rewarding side. Not only do you get the job satisfaction of leaving your victims, sorry, patients, in throbbing pain, but you can also take in a film at the same time. What should have been a 20-minute hand-and-wrist session for me on one occasion turned into a marathon. I had just settled down to watch "The Man in the Iron Mask", and the angel of misery arrived for my treatment. Unfortunately for me, "The Man in the Iron Mask" just happened to be her favourite film. Over an hour later, my session finally ended as the final titles were rolling. At the next session, I would ensure that the TV remote was at hand and the "off" button most definitely pressed before any physio began.

If it wasn't the ladies contorting my limbs at every possible and sometimes impossible angle, it was the other mob: the vampire ladies. These were not "ladies of the night" (I don't mean in that sense. Any kind of ladies were not even in my dreams at this time). I mean the vampire ladies with the trolleys who appeared only in daylight. It had taken weeks of operations and emergency surgery to have pints of blood put in my body. Now, weeks later, they sent out the vampire ladies to extract it again, syringe by syringe. They came armed with needles and said it was for testing. They had put it in there. Why test it now? Was an inferior batch used in the operating theatres?

I did have an exception to the rule, and just thinking about her now makes my face darken with the memory of it all. I was still in quite a lot of pain, but not as bad as the early days. A new nurse arrived to give me a bed bath. *That's fine*, I thought. I'd had a few of those already. She washed my face and chest with a flannel and the exposed bits of my arms. There wasn't much available to do. She then lifted the sheets back and was beginning to start on the legs.

"Whoa, there," I said. "They don't touch them."

She turned and, face smirking, replied, "Come on, Mr Church, don't be a mardy. You need to have them washed."

"No. The other nurses don't touch them; it's too painful yet."

Ignoring what I was saying, she wrung out the cloth and started to rub my leg quite briskly.

"Oh my God!" If I had the ability in me, I would have sat right up and knocked her fucking head off. I said nothing. I could do nothing but lie there helpless and at her mercy. I clenched my teeth, but there was nothing I could do to stop the tears welling and rolling down my cheeks. How I hated her at that moment. I didn't utter another word to her, and after she'd finished with my legs, she walked off with the bowl and cloth. The tears kept on rolling, and I was still gritting my teeth. My legs were throbbing with unbelievable pain.

A few minutes later, one of my familiar "angels" came over to the bed, a sister on her rounds of the ward.

"What's the matter, Dan?" she said.

A whispered "Nothing" was the reply, but she wasn't going to accept that.

All the staff were used to my chirpy banter by now, and she could tell with my face that something was amiss.

"Come on, tell me what's wrong."

"I've just had a bed bath with that new nurse, that's all, and she's done my legs. I told her not to, but she wouldn't listen."

"Oh, I see," she said as she stood really upright and pursed her lips together. "I'll be back in a moment."

She entered the small glass room at the end of the ward. At first, I couldn't hear what she was saying, but eventually, it became quite clear to everyone around.

"Have you any idea what you have just done? Do you know how much pain you would have put him through? That patient has been in here for weeks, and I assure you he is no mardy. If you'd asked any of the staff, they would have been able to tell you. Perhaps you would care to read his notes." She emphasised the word care. The sister left the glass room.

No one uttered a word, but there were a few raised eyebrows.

A couple of hours passed, and the pain in my legs had subsided to a throb. I declined painkillers when I could because I was so aware of the amounts I had taken and wanted to manage without them if possible.

The nurse, who I would have been quite happy to drown in her own bowl of soapy water, appeared at the side of my bed. She looked at me sheepishly and said, "I've just been reading your notes."

I said nothing.

"I'm so sorry... I didn't realise... I'm sorry."

Any other time, I might have put her out of her misery and said it was ok, but I didn't. I just looked at her and said nothing.

In the main, though, the nurses and therapists were a great bunch of dedicated people. I laughed and cried with them. I did rib them a lot, and sometimes I got my just deserts. I remember one day when the nurses were taking me for a shower. I had been taken for a couple of showers already, and although it was quite a performance to get me to a suitable shower room (it had to accommodate a chair), it was nice to feel clean and fresh. They would sit me on what we patients on the ward called the "bucking bronco". It was a padded seat with a hole in the centre on a tubular frame with wheels. With this contraption, you could be reasonably comfortable whilst being pushed to the shower room. It had the steering of a supermarket trolley, and a little bash on bed frames or ward doors would give you a jolt, hence the name "bucking bronco". You just had to hope you got an accomplished driver.

On this particular day, the nurses had done a fine job. They had got me gowned and ready without too much hassle, and away we went. Unfortunately, the shower room wasn't close by, which meant I had to be pushed past a few ward bays in order to get there. I had given the nurses a bit of a ribbing, which I was able to do when I was having a good day. I used to find it amusing, and usually, so did they. We had gone through our ward with only a light bash of the bronco wheels hitting a bed. I had slipped down in the seat a little, but as it was padded, I was still reasonably comfortable. Along the corridor we went and then through another ward. It was odd because I hadn't realised how popular I had become in the hospital. I had been in a long time, but as we were going through the ladies' ward, I was getting little waves from the ladies in their beds, welcoming "Hellos" and even some whistles. I couldn't believe it. I was being treated like some kind of celebrity. It did feel good to be loved.

As we reached our destination, I looked down by my side to find the best way to try to assist the nurses in preparation for my shower. It was then that I saw what had brought me so much attention. The gown had not been fastened properly and had separated at the back and risen up on either side of me. Hospital gowns seem to be designed this way in order to give as little dignity as possible to the wearer. My arse had not only been exposed to all and sundry but had also been presented squashed through the holed seat as if in a frame. What a sight. I had been pushed practically the length and breadth of the 2nd floor of the hospital with my arse on show for anyone who had cared to view it. It was hardly an exhibit for the Tate. The nurses, of course, had clocked this earlier on but put a finger to their lips as they entered each ward to ensure the patients kept stum. The laugh again was on me that day, but at least from then on, my subsequent visits to the shower were met with little muffled giggles and smiling hellos as I went through the wards. It brightened the days. After that, I always checked my gown was neatly tucked under my arse.

Without the lighter side of hospital life, my time there would have been even harder to get through. The packing and unpacking of my stomach wound was very time-consuming and stomach-churning, if you'll pardon the pun. The nurse would take off the dressing and unpack yards and yards of smelly, gunky bandage, clean up the wound and repack it with more yards of bandage. It was a horrible job for them to do, and I had more bandage used on me than Tutankhamen, except I had most of the bandage on the inside.

Gradually, the wound started to heal. The procedure of removing the various steel pins and screws was like some kind of Japanese endurance test. I had a very large pin through my knee joint from left to right. It was more like a rod, really. It held my knee in place until the joint was stable enough to have it removed.

When the day came for the removal of the pin, I was more than ready for it. The procedure commenced and involved the full weight of a hefty nurse pulling on the pin and trying to force it out through the joint. The pain was excruciating. The sight of the big, burly nurse's face was horrific. She had it screwed up tightly, and she was getting redder and redder as she pulled on the pin. She gripped the pin, and I gripped the bed to stop her from pulling me out of it. She pulled and pulled, and I yelled and yelled. Both our faces went a deep beetroot colour. The pin didn't move an inch.

"It's proving a little difficult," she said.

That was the understatement of the year.

"We'll have another go now that we've had a breather," she said. "Now, brace yourself."

She pulled again, and I braced myself again. There was still no movement.

At the end of Round 2, nurse number two entered, an even heftier nurse than the first. She obviously had more leverage to offer. I felt sure that the pin was a long way off from moving at all, never mind all the way out, but the nurse had more optimism than I had. But there again, she could afford to have. She was the one on the pulling end and not on the yelling end.

"They're not usually as tough as this," she said, "but it won't stand this kind of treatment all day. It'll have to give sooner or later."

Please, please let it be sooner, I thought.

On the third pulling, a slightly different technique was used. She brought in the gas and air in anticipation. I did use it, but I wasn't convinced it actually did anything. She braced her foot against my leg and then took hold of the pin and pulled back with all her 14-stone frame. (I may be doing her injustice with that estimate. Maybe she was 15 stone.) Her face contorted, and so did mine. We both turned beetroot red together, and I took gasps on the mask offered for the gas and air.

After over five minutes (it seemed like an eternity), a strange popping was heard and the nurse, holding the pin, shot backwards. It came out like a cork from a bottle. She held the pin aloft triumphantly. I was in bloody agony.

"I told you it wouldn't stand that all day," she said, still panting.

My knee was spurting blood from the holes where the pin had protruded. It was throbbing like hell. Thank God for modern medical techniques, which in this case seemed to be a mix of brute force and the will to succeed. I couldn't help feeling there must have been an easier way and, I'm sure, a less painful one, but as the nurse said to me afterwards, she didn't feel a thing. I now have a lot more sympathy with women in the later stages of labour. You might as well bite on a leather belt for all the good gas and air does.

The knee incident also brings to mind the day that the pins had to be removed from my wrists. They were tiny stainless steel ones, and they couldn't be seen from the outside. The heads of the pins were just below the skin. My friend Anthony had come to visit me that day. He was a big lad, well over six feet, and built like a rugby player. We were just having a laugh and a chat, and the doctor came to me and told me he wanted to remove the small pins from my wrist. Ant thought that this was his cue to leave, but the doctor had said in a matter-of-fact kind of way that there was no need and he could stay with me while he did the procedure. Ant wasn't too keen on the suggestion, but I said I wanted him to stay for a little moral support. The doctor then said he would be back with his pliers and left the ward. I looked at Ant, and he had gone ashen.

"He's only joking, Ant. Don't look so worried," I said.

"I don't think he is. He looked serious to me," he said.

I reassured him I would be anaesthetised. I was wrong. The doctor returned with his pliers. I asked him if I was going to theatre.

"No. There's no need," he replied.

Ant wanted to leave. I told him firmly that he couldn't and gave him the evil eye. He couldn't leave a friend in need.

The doctor held my wrist over the sheet, took a scalpel, and exposed the head of the pin. He gripped the pin with the pliers and pulled and twisted. Blood started to pour out of my wrist. It was very painful as my wrist was still very delicate. He tugged and twisted at the pins, and they came out one by one. Unfortunately, one of the pins snapped as he tried to take it out, and the remaining part was still in my wrist. The procedure was stopped. Anthony looked visibly shaken and was very pale. He admitted later that he thought he was going to faint.

"What happens now?" I said.

"Well, it means a trip down to theatre to remove the pin under anaesthetic."

There was a huge pool of blood on the bedsheet, and again, I was in agony and all for nothing. I still had to go down to theatre. The only positive thing I achieved from the experience was a clean sheet. I don't think Anthony found the experience rewarding in any way. We do laugh about it now, though, and I think it bonded our friendship even more. Of course, I would have made him pay at a later date if he had dared to leave me to it.

I started to quiz the doctors about my health again and got frustrated with their non-committal answers.

They would start getting exasperated and make remarks like, "Mr Church, I don't think you realise how ill you have been."

I'd been in weeks and weeks. I thought they should have some idea of when I would be well enough to be discharged. Or when I would be walking, but I didn't even get their guestimates as to how long they thought it would be. It was so very frustrating.

It is odd, but even after all I had been through, my love, well, passion for motorbikes did not waiver in the slightest. My own bike, or what was left of it, had ended up finally in a scrap yard, a mangled mess. I had hoped as I lay in the hospital that I might have been able to make a visit to the British Grand Prix at Donington Park, which was about 30 miles away. Friends had offered to take me and bring me back, but the doctors really opposed the idea. Considering my weak and unstable state at the time, it was hardly surprising that they did. I had to settle for watching it on telly.

One of the ex-patients from the hospital knew how I wanted to go, and as he had been discharged and was going to go to the GP himself, he told me he would bring me back a baseball cap as a souvenir. He was true to his promise, and I kept the cap on my bedside cabinet. It was a really treasured item. I worried about it being stolen, though, as items did have a tendency to go missing. Therefore, I decided to give the cap to Gill to take home with her.

On her next visit, she had some exciting news. She had bought a new (new to her, that is) second-hand car. Paul, my cousin who knew about cars, had given it the once over to ensure that she wasn't buying a heap. She wanted me to look at the newly acquired car. I was duly placed in a wheelchair, all waste bags, tubes and bottles attached, and pushed to the hospital car park. Gill should have had L plates on. I was banged down kerbs and pushed over bumps to view her new purchase. I looked the car over, and it seemed pretty good.

"Very nice," I said.

She looked quite proud of herself that I thought she had made a good choice. I had on my GP baseball cap and put it in the car so that Gill could take it home for safekeeping. She pushed me on another bone-shaking journey back to the ward and returned me to bed. She stayed a few more minutes and then kissed me goodbye. She had the children to pick up on the way home.

After a little while, Gill returned to the ward crying and upset. She had gone to where she had parked the car to find that there was only an empty space. Somebody had nicked the car, and even worse than that, my prized cap had gone too.

"Oh, bloody hell!" Now that *was* worth crying over.

CHAPTER 4

THE JOY AND THE PAIN

As the months passed, my main aim in life was to return home. I was still in pain and unable to walk, but eventually, the doctors let me go home for the weekends. My home, being a bungalow, was easily accessible in my wheelchair. Gill had thought it best that we had separate rooms and that I had a bedroom of my own. I still had a catheter and a colostomy bag fitted. Gill also had the children to look after and thought she needed a good night's sleep in order to cope. I was only too happy to be allowed home and would have accepted any terms in order to do that, but it would have been nice to have her at my side. It had been such a long time since I had known the comfort of her next to me, felt the warmth radiating from her body and heard her gentle breathing, but it was not to be.

The clarity of all the colours outside was amazing. That first time that I ventured around the garden in the wheelchair truly overwhelmed my senses. It was like going outside for the first time ever. The breeze blew gently on my face. The sky was a bright, bright blue, and the clouds were suspended in it like big soft pillows that I could almost touch. The colours of the trees were so vivid, the different shades of green and the textured look of the brown bark of the trunks. Birds seemed to be singing louder. The air smelled fresher. Why had I not noticed all this before? How much we take for granted. Everything seemed clearer and so much brighter. It was a spiritual moment. I promised myself not to take for granted the beauty of nature that's around me all the time.

I hated returning to hospital each week, but I was always physically shattered when I returned, and I know Gill found it difficult for me to be at home permanently. I needed too much care. I had strings of visitors each weekend, and it was so nice to chat with them in my own home. I realised what true friends meant to a person, meant to me. I had cans of Guinness bought me by the dozen. An abundance of jokes were told to me, and my friends would always ask if there was anything they could do, saying I was to let them know if there was. They meant it, too. However, I was very dependent on Gill and felt aware of the burden that I was to her. Playing with the children as best I could gave me immense pleasure. We played board games and cards and did jigsaws together. I was really eager to get back home permanently, but the doctors were still adamant that I would not walk again. Plus, as I still had the colostomy and catheter fitted, Gill did not want the responsibility of the care that I needed.

Things went reasonably well at the weekends, medically speaking. I was still feeling a little isolated from my wife, but I suppose that was understandable when you consider what I looked like. I didn't smell too good either. My tubes and attachments weren't always totally leakproof. What a mess! Could I blame her?

It was during one of these weekends I tried to do something really foolish and strictly against doctors' orders. Nevertheless, I had thought about doing it, and in my mind, it was a calculated risk. I had thought about it logically for a while now. When the nurses needed to change my sheets or transport me for x-rays, it was necessary for them to lift me onto my feet and gently twist me to sit me in a chair. The full weight of my body had never been on my feet because I was so well supported, but I did get a feel for it. I could feel my feet on the floor, and the pain in my thigh muscles as they took the strain. I could do it, I was sure. I just had to take the pain and the strain and try.

One day, when I was in the chair in the bedroom, I decided to give it a go. I chose my moment when I was feeling pretty good and Gill wasn't around. My nerves were jangling, but I'd got to try. I took the weight on the splinted arms and pushed upwards. Pain seared through my body. Perseverance was the order of the day, and persevere I did. I pushed and grimaced and clenched my teeth. Sweat poured down my face, but eureka! I found the strength. I was on my feet, very shakily, very painfully, but I was up. The tears carried on rolling down my face, but they had changed from tears of pain and effort to tears of relief. I knew I could do it. I decided that while I was up, I might as well carry on, and with the wall and furniture to help me, the first tentative step was taken. The pain was unbelievable, but it still felt right somehow. I just seemed to know it would happen. There was one step, and then I needed to try the other leg. I took another pace and then another and ventured out into the hall. I was holding onto the walls, and I felt like glass, so vulnerable and delicate. If I were to fall, I felt I would shatter like glass, too. It was odd how I could feel so strong and so weak at the same time.

It wasn't long before Gill spotted me leaning on the hall wall. Unfortunately, I had not pre-thought out my return to the wheelchair, nor the exertion the five or six steps would take. Luckily (I think), Gill had spotted me, and after giving out a high-pitched shriek, she hurtled towards me. She grabbed the chair, rushed up behind me, and with a neatly executed move, pushed the chair behind me whilst bringing the other arm in front of me. With a push on my chest, I was deposited back in the chair. A superb piece of action. She then began to bellow out a few select phrases, punctuated with a few expletives. I can't remember exactly what, but I do know she thought I was some kind of idiot and then threatened me with what the doctors would do to me when they found out just what kind of idiot I was. Anyway! Whatever it was, I couldn't care less. I had walked. Everyone said it couldn't be done, but I proved them wrong. I could walk. Wow! That day was the most momentous of my recovery.

I tried walking more often after that. With backup, of course. The doctors were amazed and agreed they really didn't know anymore what my limitations would be, if any. I decided to use my own judgement, just like I had been doing so far, really.

The time came when I was going to go home permanently. I was due to go home at teatime. Anthony had other plans, though. He'd come to see me at visiting time in the afternoon, and as I was due to go home later that day anyway, he decided to take me there and then. I had received my medication from the pharmacy, and away we went. Gill would be surprised when we got home a few hours ahead of schedule. I had a frame on wheels to cradle my urine bag. I wore loose clothing in order to fit over my various tubes and bags. The most comfortable clothing I found was a big V-neck knitted cricket jumper and a long pair of roomy Bermuda cotton shorts. I was a sight to behold, but at least I was going home.

We pulled up the drive, and when we got to the front door, we were met by a very surprised Gill, who said rather abruptly, "What are you doing here?"

Hardly the reception I expected. Little did I know that I had surprised her alright. She had planned a surprise party for me and was in the middle of baking cakes and sorting everything out. Anthony was told to "Get rid of him somewhere" for a couple of hours. Balloons and banners needed to be hung, and there was still lots to do. Anthony had managed to put a spanner in the works by bringing me home too soon.

I didn't want to have a look at the house round the corner his mate was buying, but I had to go. It wasn't what I'd got in mind on my first day home. Any amount of protesting didn't change his mind. I had to be pushed up the road to the bungalow. I could blooming well whack him at times.

I knew there was something happening, but I didn't expect what I saw on my return home. There were cars parked all the way up the drive, all over the front lawn and around the back.

I walked through the front door and was met with, "Surprise, surprise!"

The hall, living room and stairs were thronged with family and friends, holding glasses and aiming party poppers. There were balloons adorning the ceiling, and

I hadn't realised how many friends I had. It was great, if not a bit daunting. I was still a little embarrassed about my appearance and the tubes and bags that accompanied me everywhere I went, but they didn't seem to notice. If they were shocked by my appearance (all seven stone of me), then they didn't show it. The first hour I enjoyed. The second hour was a strain, and I was just about done in by the third hour. I was well and truly knackered. I was really touched by the response from my friends, though.

It would be good to be home permanently. I felt more than ready as six months had passed since the accident. Gill, I know, had mixed feelings about me returning home. Although I would have struggled to manage without her during that time, I also sensed a significant difference in the feelings she had for me. She never expressed them verbally at that point, but I felt lonely with her sometimes, and I had the feeling she wanted to be somewhere else. I longed for her to give me a kiss or a cuddle, but we were both in our own little worlds. She had to overcome her sense of insecurity about me not being there to pay the bills, and I was unable to offer her any practical or emotional support. She had to learn how to juggle finances as well as looking after children, the home and an invalid husband. For Gill, it was overload time. She coped the best she could with all the practical things, but could not cope any more emotionally and would not cope. She had had enough.

I was never to get the closeness, respect, or love back from Gill ever again.

Although months had passed since the accident, the repercussions were still resonating, still hitting hard throughout different aspects of my life, like never-ending waves. I had returned home a different man, and Gill was a different woman. We shared no warmth, although I longed for it. I didn't feel worthy of it, however, and asking her for love: a kiss, a cuddle, or even for her to hold my hand was inconceivable. I'd hoped that she would want to hold me. Just once, maybe, but it never happened. I leant forward for a kiss once. I thought the moment was right, but I obviously misread the situation. Gill leant backwards as I went forwards and then got up from the settee very quickly. She said she had a cold, and it was best not to, and then she scuttled off into the kitchen to put the kettle on. She washed, and she cleaned the home. She looked after the children, and she looked after me, but I could almost feel her cringing at the sight of me. I never was to sleep with my wife again, let alone make love to her.

The return home was not the realisation of the big dream. I had overcome a big physical battle, but an even bigger emotional one was about to commence. Things were very, very different. Little did I know, at this time, that they would never be the same again.

CHAPTER 5

RETURN OF FAITH?

Periodically, I was having meetings at home with my solicitor, but I had a bad feeling about it. I had already been told that the lady driving the car would not be prosecuted for dangerous driving. That bit I could maybe understand. I thought she would probably admit her decision to pull out had resulted in horrific consequences that day, and that would be hard enough for anyone to live with. Perhaps the police thought she would suffer all her life anyway, living with the consequences of her actions. But that wasn't the case. She didn't admit anything. She didn't give any apologies or offer any explanation to anyone; however, the police had decided not to prosecute. They had no idea the effect that decision would have on Matt's family and on me.

For his mum and dad, there was no acknowledgement of the wrong she had committed that day, albeit by accident, but it needed to be told. His mum and dad needed to know why, and I needed them to know it wasn't me. It wasn't my lack of judgement that caused their son to lose his life that day. His parents had, understandably, so much grief, losing a son, just barely an adult whose whole life should have been ahead of him. They would never attend his wedding or see his children/their grandchildren. They had suffered such a loss. Didn't the police realise who the real victims were in this? An excited young man had gone out for a ride with a friend one sunny spring day, and he never came home. Parents, girlfriend, family and friends would never see him again. The police, in their wisdom, deemed that the woman who pulled out in front of the bike that day had suffered enough. The police had no idea… Matt's family were left to pick up the pieces of their lives and were left devastated. Suffered? Ask them what suffering is. With not so much as an apology or a proper explanation as to why.

Ian and Emma still visited me and were great; no recriminations from them. Ian told me that his parents were emotionally struggling, his mum especially. Maybe they thought I'd been speeding. I had ridden away from their house with a quick burst on the accelerator, after all. I wished it felt right for me to talk to his parents, but it didn't. I wished I could tell them I had done everything I could in the split second I had to avoid the crash, but I couldn't tell them. It would have been purely a selfish act, and I so desperately wanted to do so. I wanted them to tell me it was ok and that it wasn't my fault. It was an accident. Something out of my control. This was the thing I needed so much, and yet it would have only been for my benefit, I know. I wanted to tell them how sorry I was. That I would have given my life to spare him if I could. That I would have gone with him and walked hand in hand with him on to wherever it is that comes after death... if I could. If only I could turn back time!

In my dreams, I could do it. I could approach his mum and tell her I'm sorry. I'm sorry he's gone and that I would have saved him if I could. If it was in my earthly power to do so, I would have saved him. Then, with her arms enveloped around me, she would tell me it was ok. She would reassure me it wasn't my fault and that she didn't blame me. We could share a moment, share our grief, and reach for comfort in the arms of each other. That was my selfish dream. One I yearned for; I still do.

The driver and the police denied us that in their ignorance, and they probably won't ever realise. I will now never have complete closure. I can't approach Matt's mum and ask for it now. I will probably go to my grave wondering how much she blames me. Does she forgive me for agreeing to take him that day? I don't know. I can't completely forgive myself. I live with it. It's my cross.

I didn't experience any afterlife experiences on the two occasions I died in the ambulance or in the twilight weeks in hospital. No pearly gates. No winged angels or harp-playing cherubs. There was nothing. I'd blamed God, and I'd challenged him in the hospital and even pleaded with him. There was nothing. The only reasoning I have on it is that maybe the dreams I had before my accident did seem like some kind of warning, but what was the point of that if I couldn't do anything about it? I also know, and somehow, it makes me feel a little easier that Matt had changed the day and the time that we had set off on that day. I hadn't chosen it. Some of my family and friends have told me that they thought it was his fate rather than mine. Maybe I was the "escort" "chosen" for the job. Perhaps this is from the belief that some people have. For some reason unknown to me, God sometimes seems fit to take the good when they are young, capturing their souls at the very pinnacle of their prime, where they are immortalised at that moment for all time. Matt stays forever 18. He was young, full of life with plans and expectations for his future, fresh, hopeful and full of optimism. He will forever remain in my thoughts like that. He will never be middle-aged or old. Never feel the tragedy and heartache of losing a close loved one as the family he left behind have. Never know the feeling of having optimism dashed or of failing in any way, of running out of time for the things he wanted to achieve. Or ever have the fear of feeling he let his family down without ever having time to rectify things or change them. He left this world young, vital and innocent, unmarked by the stains that life can put on a soul. He carried the hopefulness of youth with him, maybe into the hereafter. I hope so. Where he will remain like that, bringing a breath of fresh air to the old souls up there, raising a smile like he used to for me. I hope that's how it is.

Maybe I was just the messenger. I am not sure I feel it as some kind of faith returning. I know I don't blame God anymore. I now won't change my mind on a journey once I have made my arrangements, though. I don't believe that has anything to do with faith; it is more like superstition. God… if there is one, has shown me nothing but contempt. Had he listened to me when I had begged him to help out? Had he bugger! That is what I thought. I'm a little more relaxed with it now, and I can let it be. I don't search for answers anymore; life just seems to happen. When I reflect on my lot now, it's not too bad! I am mainly at peace with myself, but it is a point that took some getting to. It has taken years and changed me into the man I am. Maybe telling my story might help some other poor soul who has been unfortunate to go through a similar situation. If it does, then I'm glad.

I did get a visit to my home one day from a worried-looking middle-aged lady. I knew who she was. She lived up the road. She asked if she could come in. She looked so troubled, and she asked if I would do something for her. I replied I would if I could. She wanted me to go and see her son. He was at home recovering from a motorbike crash, but she explained that recovery was slow and he was beginning to give up on life. His legs were smashed and not recovering at the rate he wanted them to. She said he was getting depressed. She wanted me to talk to him to see if I could help.

I visited him. I told him what had happened to me and how long I had been in the hospital, and I showed him a photo of when I had come out weighing seven stones. I relayed to him that doctors said I would never walk again, and that I held the record for the man who had received the most pints of blood and still survived. I explained it had been a hard journey, but I came out of the other side. We also had a bit of banter; we laughed together, and I left. His mother whispered thank you as I did so. I think it helped. I hope so.

I still had a long and gruelling battle with litigation ahead of me. My solicitor was fighting the car driver's motor insurance company for compensation, but they were digging their heels in. We had a real fight on our hands. The police's decision not to prosecute the driver meant that my case was all the more difficult. I'd been on really good wages working for a private colliery, and then suddenly, I was relying on DHSS benefits. Gill was distraught most of the time, filling in more forms, applying for free school lunches, school uniform grants, etc., etc. Money was really tight, and I couldn't help her. I couldn't help anyone. In fact, I was an extra burden. I still needed nursing, and tending to my physical needs caused a lot of work. Sheets needed changing, catheter bags emptied, I needed washing and dressing, and my wounds needed packing. I knew she looked at me in a different way now. I thought of myself differently, too, so I could hardly blame her. I think she would have found it easier if I had still been in hospital. She wasn't callous enough to tell me that, but I knew. I wasn't about to give her the easy option, though. I'd spent long enough in the hospital, and I didn't want to go back.

She used to take a couple of hours out here and there. I didn't know where she went, but I knew she needed the break. I didn't ask her. I was still so grateful that she was putting up with me and looking after me. I didn't think I deserved it. I didn't think I deserved any warmth of human kindness. I didn't deserve it, and what's more, I didn't get it either. I was an emaciated, smelly heap of a husband.

Don't get me wrong: Gill looked after my physical needs very well, although she couldn't hide the distaste she had for doing some of the jobs she did for me. I could see it on her face when she washed around the catheter pipes or other things she considered as equally gruesome. She'd had some training regarding the medical help

I would need. She abhorred it, and I could see it in her face: she would rather the district nurses do the tasks.

I had spent months in hospital, fighting a losing battle to keep some kind of dignity. As the medical staff were so busy, the variety and nature of all my injuries meant that it wasn't always practical to do so. Additionally, it isn't one of the priorities when tight schedules have to be kept. Therefore, I desperately needed to get back to some kind of home where my "loving" wife could tend to me. It would have been so much better for me. However, the effect of going home probably added more quickly to the breakdown of my family life and my marriage. I just didn't want any doctors and nursing staff around more than I needed to, but I think I should have been more understanding of Gill's needs. All people are different, and Gill wasn't the martyr kind. No way could she even contemplate compromising herself that much as to become a nurse for me. She had never done that role, and she wasn't about to start then. She needed a lot more input from me. For there to be any chance of us to survive, I needed to get some income again and at least some resemblance of the physical body I used to have. Anyone taking one look at me would know not to "hold their breath" on that score.

The nights could be quite long, lying there in my son's bedroom while my wife slept in our bedroom. She said she needed to cope with a lot of things through the day (me being one of the things). Therefore, a good night's sleep was important, and sleeping with me and my pipes wouldn't give her that. Just sometimes, though, I would have loved for her to lie at the side of me so that we could hug each other a little, but I knew she would find that idea far too distasteful.

I needed to get better, and quickly, if I was going to build bridges to help our relationship. There was once during this time that I awoke in horrific pain down in my bladder area. The pain was excruciating. My bladder felt like it was at bursting point. My genitals (what was left of them) were on fire. I needed to take out the catheter. The urine seemed to be backing up in the pipe. I yanked at the tube. What pain! But it remained in place. I shouted at Gill to get some scissors. She came running into the bedroom, and she soon became very aware of what I wanted to do. She went out into the hall to phone the doctor.

"Get the scissors!" I shouted.

"Oh, no!" she said. "You can't cut it, Dan. You'll be in trouble."

"I've got more trouble than I can cope with now. Fetch the bloody scissors!"

She ran into the kitchen and fetched the scissors from the kitchen drawer. She slapped them in my hand and shouted, "Well, you do it then! I'm not doing it."

It didn't concern me who did it as long as it was done. With one snip of the pipe, it was done, and it was instant relief. The pipe whiplashed the air; there was so much pressure behind it. Urine in the pipe shot everywhere, but I didn't care. With a sigh of relief, I laid back onto the mattress, leaving Gill with yet another mess to clean up.

The doctor arrived and explained that I was making a lot of calcium and that it had blocked my tube, causing the urine to back up. Unfortunately, I did have to have another one fitted. My bladder was still far too weak to work properly.

Friends visited, bearing gifts and cans of Guinness, and were still very welcome. These visits brought a happy intervention to my day. My cousin Paul lived around the corner, and we would hold wheelchair competitions. I was very proficient at handling and twisting and turning in it at this stage. He'd jokingly order me out of the chair so that he could have a go. He'd then dump me on a comfy chair while he 'wheelied' and raced down the hall.

"Beat that, then," he'd say.

He'd put me back in, and then it would be my turn to show him what I could do: great fun.

Although we were cousins, we had been brought up quite close and were more like brothers. Neither of us had a real brother, but we had one older sister each. Paul's passion had always been fast cars and mine motorbikes, and when we were younger, we weren't averse to trying to scare each other shitless. I sat in the passenger seat of his Ford Mexico while he spun it around corners, causing the tyres to screech, trying to get me to admit to being scared while I hung onto the seat. I then used to take him for the "ride of his life" as my pillion passenger on my bike. We were young and indestructible. Stupid idiots, more like, but apart from the odd minor crashes and scrapes, we came through it unscathed. It seems funny that a few years later, going at what turned out to be a steady 45 miles an hour caused such devastation. That's how it happens, I suppose.

CHAPTER 6

PROGRESS

More and more legal liaising between myself and the police and the solicitor was taking place, especially as I was getting stronger and able to cope with the memories better. The police were not very sympathetic and seemed to have created their own version of what happened that day and the cause of the accident. They had already made up their mind it was the "wild, fast biker" who was to blame. I was furious with them.

I instructed my solicitor to have an independent engineer's report done on my bike and get the scene of the accident information. My bike, I had been told, was at a local salvage yard and was a total wreck, but still in the same condition as when they had taken delivery of it. My solicitor advised me against the independent report I was requesting, but I couldn't understand why. Then he dropped the bombshell. I never forgave him for it.

"The trouble with getting your own report done, though, Dan, means that it could be used as evidence against you."

"What do you mean?" I said.

"Well, it will be there in black and white. The condition of your bike before the crash. Any faults will be reported, and also the speed you were travelling."

I couldn't believe it. "What the hell are you talking about, Tomlinson? All these weeks, I have been telling you I did nothing wrong. My bike WAS roadworthy, and I WASN'T speeding. I have nothing to hide." *What the fuck…?* "If YOU don't believe me, and you're my solicitor, how the hell do you expect anyone else to? I don't want you on my case anymore. Get Mr Kieran to get someone else. You're done."

He was done, too. I phoned Kieran and Kieran and, in no uncertain terms, told them to get someone else onto it, pronto. Mr Jim Kieran himself came, and it took a hell of a time for him to unruffle my feathers.

Engineers were appointed to do a thorough report. It took a few weeks to complete, but it came back. The report was very thorough, and it stated, in black and white, like I knew it would, that my bike was in excellent condition and perfectly maintained. When the crash had occurred, my headlight had been on. I always travelled this way because it made for better visibility. All the adjustments on the bike were just as they should have been. I KNEW my stuff. They estimated the speed I was travelling was approximately 45 miles an hour and not above 50 miles an hour. *Stuff that in your pipe and smoke it, Tomlinson.*

Jim Keiran, I liked. He was a middle-aged man with a lot of experience. He seemed gentle and was quietly spoken. In all the time I knew him, I never saw him agitated or ruffled. At times, when I got upset or angry with talking about the past events, he remained in control, which seemed to soothe me. He let me talk a lot, and he listened to me. Yes, Mr Kieran, Jim, was ok. I could work with him.

My health progressed slowly; my legal case progressed slowly, too. I needed to prove the accident wasn't my fault. Until then, I didn't realise that was something I had to verify. When I had proven my innocence, I then had to put a case forward to sue the car driver's insurance company. I needed money to live on, to support my family and to help me out before I was well enough to return to work. At least, that is what I thought back then. Little did I know just what a long battle I had on my hands.

Progress on my health and the legal case was slow going, but at least it was a big improvement compared to what my love life was doing. Gill seemed to be growing more and more distant from me. I saw her doing practical jobs, such as nursing me, and domestic chores, and the time she put into looking after the children and cleaning the house. Emotionally, I wouldn't know she was there at all. We hardly ever conversed except for the latest updates on what the DHSS were doing or not doing for us, and then there'd be tears. She was getting to the end of her tether. She would get emotional over our financial predicament, but she never seemed to have any positive emotion towards me. We'd not really discussed the prognosis for the sexually physical side of my recovery, and to be honest, I pushed it to the back of my mind.

I was still having too many outpatient visits to the hospital, and as I had spent so much time there, I hated going. I had concentrated so much on getting through the pain and back on my feet that it had not been a paramount issue at the beginning. I had lost a testicle and the other one was badly damaged. Thankfully, everything returned to the correct size a few weeks after the accident, but my pelvis had taken a huge battering, having hit the petrol tank first. The groin area of my body had taken all the impact of the tank.

The wire that Mr Scott, the surgeon, had threaded around my pelvis to pull it together and hold it in place was still in situ. It seemed to have settled in there and so was left untouched. My scrotum was somewhat saggy, having nothing in it, and my penis didn't look too bad, but it did show some signs of battle. There were some suture scars around the middle of it. *It kind of added to the character,* I thought. I always joked afterwards that the surgeon had thought it such a fine piece that he cut a few inches out of the middle. Somewhere, a surgeon was knocking around the Royal Hospital with a 10-incher obtained through the unsavoury misuse of the scalpel and knife. Whether or not all the tackle would work, God only knew. I knew it better had in time because I knew Gill wouldn't want to just sit and admire the newly acquired look, even if it did mean enhanced character.

I had a deep crevice above my right side where an amount of remodelling had occurred as a result of the necrotic flesh around the wound being cut away. There was no soft bit of flesh on my right hip, but just a ridge of bone covered by tight skin. It didn't look as bad as it felt, though. It felt like a tin plate. The doctors at the hospital asked whether I wanted to try some hormone inserts pushed into my stomach as I wouldn't be making enough testosterone. I didn't even want to discuss it. I didn't believe it was the time or the place to talk about that subject content with them. It was far too early, and it was something for me and Gill to discuss in our own time. What I didn't realise was that Gill had a different line on it than me. However, as we weren't really singing from the same hymn sheet, she was just thinking I was some selfish chauvinist pig who wasn't even going to let her have her say on the matter. I suppose she was right. It wasn't open for discussion, especially with the doctors who had already got so close on the physical side of me that every body part and orifice had been invaded, piped, poked, cleaned, stuffed, injected, bandaged, splintered or plastered. I couldn't stand the thought of laying myself bare, either physically or emotionally, to discuss any possible sexual failings. Not bloody likely. I wasn't up to it then, and I wasn't sure if ever I would be. Subject closed! Another nail in the coffin for me and Gill.

Saturation point had been reached. I wanted time. Time to be left at peace, to catch my breath. I wanted to get back a little that I had taken so much for granted before the accident. I yearned for my family, my home and peace: to have things like they used to be. No invasions from the outside world. No doctors or nurses. No police and solicitors. No terrible memories coming to the fore of my mind, such as Matt sailing over my head and hitting the hard road and the imagined look on the faces of Matt's parents when they had the news broken to them of their young son's death. What a wedding memory for Ian and Emma to be stopped at the airport on their way to what should have been their honeymoon and should have been the happiest day of their lives. If only there was some way of blocking it all out, everything for just a while.

The physical pain was tough to cope with, but the guilt had the result of making me feel and look completely wretched.

The days kept going by. No stopping them, either. Not all days were bad ones. I still thought the nature I could see in my own back garden was awesome. I still delighted in hearing the robin chirping and watching the little wrens darting in and out of the peony bush that grew at the base of the silver birch near the front window. The kids were my saving grace, too. Their innocence and youthful enthusiasm for everyday life provided a good stabiliser when I felt I was too far into the black abyss.

It's all very well saying you can't cope with life. What is the alternative? For most ordinary people, you do cope, for the simple reason there is no other choice. Life seems unbearable, but it never stops running on, and you get through it day by day. There was an option, I suppose. You could always end it all. Yes! A full bottle of paracetamol and a bottle of Jack Daniels would do it. But that was not an option, as far as I was concerned. Well, maybe the once when I was in hospital begging for the shotgun. However, even during my lowest ebb, or at any time after that, I would not have contemplated it. Well, I don't think so. Maybe time has a way of fading those blackest of moments. Thank goodness. My family, kids, Mum and Dad, sister and all my friends had shown me so much support and love; I couldn't let them down by adding that to their lives.

There was also the possibility that I could lose my mind and be dragged away in a straitjacket to a mental hospital somewhere to talk to squirrels and 6-foot-tall white rabbits; to exist in a hazy, subliminal world called 'ga ga' land. Will it as you may, however, that does not happen as a result of your own volition. You have to crack up, and who knows who has the say and timings over whether or not that is going to happen? So, when people say, "Oh! How did you get through it?" The answer has got to be that you don't have a choice or a hand in it, really. You just do, and the days keep on coming.

The children were great. They just carried on doing what they do best... being children. They squabbled and giggled and played and ate and slept. All three of them were quite small for their ages, and they looked like little cherubs. I wished I could have provided for them better and treated them to things from time to time. My son was really young, but Gemma and Rachel, my girls, had been having horse-riding lessons before the "day", and Gemma had begun to pester Gill and me for a pony. It would not happen in her wildest dreams now. In fact, we couldn't even afford the lessons anymore. She had also attended dance classes. She showed quite a talent for dancing, and we had seen her a few times in dance shows on local stages. We still managed to scrape together the money for the class fees, but when it came to the time to buy new dance outfits or shoes, it was always a struggle. Luckily, my mum helped out where she could with little contributions, offering money for Rachel's Brownie outfits and school trips.

Because my son was younger, keeping him happy was still pretty cheap and simple. He was content with a new little toy car to play with and playing a board game around the table. Wouldn't it be wonderful if every aspect of your life could be as easy as that?

Gill was quite happy for me to participate with the kids whenever I was able. This meant she could have a little time to do something else. We never did things as a family anymore. If I was ok and entertaining the kids, then that was her cue to go out of the way.

The rush of friends that had visited me in the few weeks after my coming home had died down to a much steadier level. All of them were still calling and helping out, but at a slower pace.

One particular friend was still calling around quite often. He was more a friend of my cousin Paul's, really, but he and his wife had gone out with us a couple of times, and therefore, Gill and I had got to know him quite well, too. His name was also Paul, and we had always distinguished this Paul from Cousin Paul by calling him "Ugly Paul". Not that he was particularly ugly, but my cousin Paul had what women would call "dishy good looks." It had been my luck in our younger days to have "dishy" Paul as my cousin and 'going out friend' because I knew he would attract the girls' attention. He had dark hair and blue eyes with a cheeky twinkle in them. The girls couldn't resist his charm. I was the taller and, may I add, the fitter, "distinguished" one. Anyway, we got a lot of attention from the girls when we went out together. Perhaps we should have called Cousin Paul "pretty" and the other one just Paul, but anyway, I digress.

Ugly Paul would visit us on many occasions, and I quite enjoyed his company, but I was a little mystified as to why he had seemed to take to us so much. His wife, Kate, sometimes came with him, but mainly, he would call on his own. To be honest, I did have some suspicions of his intentions quite early on, but I dismissed them as thoughts of an insecure husband who, at that moment in time, hadn't got a lot going for him. I noticed how giggly Gill seemed to get in his presence and how his arrival would bring a little glow to her face. Gill had always had a bit of a flirty nature, though, and men found her attractive. It was always harmless and just a facet of her bubbly, outgoing nature.

She was a petite blonde with a likeable, sociable nature. She was a good housewife in the main and a good mother. She could get to be a little flighty from time to time, but she had given birth to Gemma not a year after we had been married and had the other two kids in quick succession. We had planned this so that in our forties, we would still be young enough to enjoy ourselves. That was our plan, at least. However, having the kids young meant that sometimes she would feel a little trapped and want a bit of freedom. A good laugh and a night out with the girls would be needed. She would sometimes need that new dress she couldn't do without, even though I could hardly scrape the money together for the gas bill. If I were to say no, it could result in endless howling and sulking. She would tell me what a mean husband I was, and eventually, I would be worn down and I'd hand her the money. Her face would light up as if I'd given her the world. I would be left grumpier knowing I was even further away from paying the gas bill. It didn't happen every day though. She would cook regular meals for me, and all in all, she was quite a good wife. The fact she was so small had been an asset. She was a good pillion passenger and not at all "girly".

I thought we did pretty well together as a team. It came as a surprise, therefore, to find out later that some of my family and friends had declared after the accident that they didn't expect Gill to stay with me. I was the surprised one. I thought she would.

On one occasion, Ugly Paul visited, and I was asleep in my room. After hearing voices, I decided to see who was there and got in my wheelchair to have a look in the room. I was a little surprised to see Paul and Gill sitting together on the settee. They both looked sheepish when I entered the living room, and Gill jumped up, offering an immediate explanation. Too immediate for my liking.

"Paul's dropped in to see us," she said.

"So I see," was my reply.

"He's not been here long. You were asleep, so we didn't want to wake you."

I thought that very odd, especially as the coffee cups on the table had telltale stained rings around the inside, showing that the coffee dregs in them were far from fresh. Alarm bells began to ring, but maybe I was wrong with what I was thinking. I convinced myself that was the case, as it meant I wouldn't have to deal with more complications in my life.

When Paul visited after that, I kept an eye on both Gill and Paul when they were together and I saw the odd smile or a quick glance exchanged between them. I still wasn't sure, but I had enough doubt in my mind to start to think: *What if? What if Gill was to leave me? What would happen to the kids and to me? It would mean me losing the kids and only seeing them at weekends. Where would I live? Paul was younger and fitter and had more prospects for the future. He had a job and everything going for him. Above all, he could offer a fully active sex life. The most fundamental requisite of being married.* But just maybe I was imagining it.

The pressure we'd both been under had been such that I was feeling useless. It had been months since the accident, and yet I still couldn't walk except for a few paces. Inactivity, lack of exercise and constant supply of good meals had certainly had an effect on my body. I had gained stones in weight, but the lack of exercise meant that I was looking quite flabby and not at all toned. I hadn't worried too much at the time because I was concentrating on getting through the more immediate physical problems like being pain free and being able to walk. My appearance was not my primary concern. Friends and family were only too encouraging when they saw that my weight was increasing from the puny seven stone I was when arriving back home from hospital.

When I eventually did take stock of myself, it made me realise I hadn't got a lot to offer Gill. I was no match for a rival. I had nothing to fight with. Even then, I was subconsciously taking it for granted that love, loyalty and respect may not have a part in what was considered essential in a marriage, as far as Gill would be concerned. One day soon, I was going to face up to the fact that I may hear some news that I wouldn't like. I had really irrational thoughts on possible outcomes. Thoughts that I am quite embarrassed to relay. *Gill might stay. Perhaps for the kids, if not for me. If I turned a blind eye to what I suspected was going on, then maybe she would be happy with an affair. Gill and Paul could continue with an affair, which would be a release from me. It would give her some respite from all the stress I brought to her life and would obviously tend to her other physical needs. She could then come home to me.* What kind of thoughts are those for a husband to have? I barely thought about it consciously, but I have no doubt that somewhere, lurking in a corner of my brain, I thought it could be a feasible solution. When I try to rationalise it now, I know it was complete madness, contemplated as a result of feeling inadequate and desperate.

The walls of my son's bedroom were oh so familiar to me now. The baseball design on the duvet cover. The box of toys in the corner. I would squeeze my eyes tightly together to stop the tears from trickling down my cheeks. Sometimes I would stare at an object in the darkness. Maybe the silhouette of my son's teddy bear. I'd use it as a focal point to stare at. If I concentrated on something specific, I could then block out a multitude of other things. I could stop reliving the accident or the painful thoughts of what Matt's last moments were like. I was so tired of the pain in my back, head and legs. I would try to block out my pain, both physical and emotional. To add to my list of things to worry about was now the question: *What do I do about Gill?*

To be honest, after a while, it wasn't that hard. I decided not to think about it, full stop. What will be will be and I didn't have any control over it and just maybe I was wrong.

I also was trying to practise the master plan I had devised in hospital. I played with the children when I could. I tried not to be too big a burden to Gill. I got on my feet every day and took more steps around my home. I still felt that I was made of glass when I was on my feet, but I was making progress. I still had friends calling and lifting my spirits. My cousin still cut my grass, and my mum helped with the housework. Money was still very tight, and we seemed to be ever fighting with the various departments of the social services for essentials such as food, clothes, help with council tax, etc. Gill would show her despair in the day with outbursts of tears and sometimes let her frustrations out by bellowing at the kids. I would try to reassure Gill that things would get better when I was well enough to return to work.

My despair I felt on my own at night when sometimes my resolve would weaken and silent tears would be shed. To let Gill see me would only add to the feeling of inadequacy I had about myself. No mortgage repayments were being paid, and there was hardly enough food on the table. I was still being nursed. I had poor control over my bodily functions and not even any stirrings of a sexual nature. It was a wonder she'd not left me already. We continued to play-act our way through the marriage.

CHAPTER 7

TAKING ACTION

Ugly Paul was still making his regular visits. He was really pleasant and showed me lots of attention, but I'd no doubt he was showing my wife more. There were still continuous outpatient visits to the hospital. Lots of them because there were so many different departments involved. One to check my neurological responses as I had landed on my bonce. It had taken weeks for the impression of the inside of my helmet to disappear from my face. In the early days, I had huge bruises that covered a big proportion of my face. All outward signs on my face and head had disappeared, but it was feared that the impact could have left me with some kind of brain damage or maybe the chance I could develop epileptic fits. The longer I was clear, the more remote the possibility of developing them. The more time that passed, therefore, the more optimistic the doctors were that fits would not be a problem. Good news there, then.

I did have to have my short-term memory tested. This involved having to be put through a number of seemingly silly tests. Counting backwards in threes from one hundred was one of them. Remembering items on a tray after a length of time was another. The "nut" doctors could deduce from all these tests that I had lost ten percent of my short-term memory through brain cell damage. I still find this piece of deduction pretty amazing when they had no benchmark to work from. How did they know what kind of brain capacity I had before? Anyway, it turns out that I'm only a 90 percenter. The only evidence I had of this myself was the fact that I couldn't seem to remember shopping list items or what the kids might need for school, such as PE kits. Lists were therefore made and added to throughout the week in order to remind me. I diarised appointments for doctors and hospitals and added them to a kitchen calendar for daily referral. This element of my injuries didn't have too big an impact on my life. In fact, whilst I completed the silly tests, apparently Gill was doing them herself in her head, and even she admitted that I sometimes completed the tasks quicker than she did. Einstein, eat your heart out. Maybe I could have made a rocket scientist if I'd applied myself more before the accident. It would have made a change from my mining job.

I visited Mr Scott for the checking of my bones. I was improving more and more with my walking, but I was still in a lot of pain. My left leg is slightly bowed. I had broken it, but on my admittance to hospital, the medical staff had concentrated on life-saving procedures, and the fact I had a broken leg was not picked up immediately. This resulted in it being set a little skew whiff. My foot had no sensations in it and was "dropped" as I walked. The muscles in the foot were unable to take the weight, which resulted in me slapping it down a little with each step rather than being able to place it down. My toenails had to be removed on numerous occasions to give me some relief because they had grown thick and yellow and grew into my toes. I walked with a limp owing to the damage to the hips and pelvis. Some of the fingers on my right hand were rotated, so when I try to clench a fist, they slip on the top of each other. My wrists bore horrible scarring as a result of the number of operations involved in mending the bones. My right shoulder was dropped and pushed into my neck, so it looked a shorter length than my left. My back, although still very painful, didn't look too bad visually. The right kneecap moved from side to side. The rib cage was not too bad, either, as long as you didn't run your fingers along it because then you could tell that some ribs were at odd angles. I was a bit of a mess all round, skeletally speaking. The nose was still good. Strong and aquiline as always. What luck!

However, Mr Scott was astounded and pleased as hell to find that I could walk. Against all odds, I could get about under my own steam and was still improving all the time. He had done an amazing job. The Scott wire still looped around my pelvis didn't give me any additional problems for being left in there. The scars gave me gyp, but mainly because of the number of times the surgeons had opened them up for access. Shame we can't have zips fitted. They looked quite ugly. I had one stretching the length of my abdomen, which disappeared into my pubic hair. I had another crossing over my stomach and a strange-looking hole which looked like an extra belly button. That is where the dead flesh was cut away from my stomach. It took a long time to heal, but it left me with a little well.

I hated the visits. All the getting undressed and the prodding and the probing. The questions and then the waiting. I had spent enough time in the hospital and didn't want to go back. The visits would bring back all the memories of the terrible times of pain I had in there.

However, I did make a concerted effort to see a particular department that I wouldn't have even contemplated when first suggested. The fact that I had still got the Gill and Paul problem looming over me like a cloud prompted me into action. Gill had approached me a few times about how important it was to her to get the physical side of our relationship back. I had dismissed even thinking about it at first, but I did eventually realise that if I had any chance of keeping Gill, I'd better get back into action somehow. I'd bitten the bullet and agreed to an appointment at the willy department. God! I couldn't wait. The ultimate sacrifice.

I hoped the visit would not be in vain. I had to psyche myself up for the humiliation and embarrassment. Willy department, here I come.

The appointment at the hospital seemed to come around so quickly, but it turned out to be more of a clinical procedure rather than an emotional one. It involved having a slit in my abdomen, and then a yellowish-coloured capsule was rammed into the gap. I just had the sensation of something being forced down under my skin, and that was it. A couple of little stitches to pull the skin back together, then that was it.

It turned out to be a complete waste of time. Nothing ever came of it. It is rather an odd thing to judge, however. There had been no sexual stirrings in me whatsoever, and then, all of a sudden, I felt I was expected to spring into action. How long was it before it was supposed to take effect? The expectations just added to my stress of having to "perform". Nothing happened... two weeks after... three months after. Nothing!! I think Gill got the idea I somehow had a choice in the matter and wouldn't try. She, in turn, seemed as cold as ice regarding any affection from me. Our relationship seemed to revolve around my needs and her taking care of the kids and the house. We were both lonely, and I know it seems selfish to say, but I needed her more than she needed me. I couldn't look after myself. I wondered how much time we had left.

Although my walking had improved, I could only walk a little way on my gutter crutches. After trying to sit on my push bike one day and giving it a go, I discovered it was much less painful to pedal than it was to walk. *Great! Another step forward.* Every day from then on, I would pedal my bike around the bungalow. There was a continuous path all the way around, but I had to be careful near one end where it was a tight squeeze in between the garage and the house wall. One or two circuits were the most I could complete at first, but then, as my strength improved, I could do six or seven. What the neighbours thought, I don't know. A hamster in a wheel springs to mind. A mad hamster, maybe. Strangely enough, though, I felt completely chuffed with every additional circuit I managed to pedal. My Everest!

Although to a lot of people, I may not have looked as if I was progressing much, every slight improvement gave me great satisfaction. I still felt I might one day go back to work.

Meanwhile, Ugly Paul was still making his visits, and I was still discovering part-filled cups of cold coffee left on the table in the living room. I gave up asking Gill why she didn't call me when he had arrived so we could all chat together, but the stock answer was that she didn't want to wake me.

CHAPTER 8

MOVING ON

The litigation side of my case was also running slowly. I was asked to make a statement on just about everything. Not just what happened in the accident, but what I was like before the accident and information on my wages and potential earnings. Employers were asked about my probable future earnings, and Gill was asked to provide hers. The letters and statements were dealt with, and then there would be nothing for ages, just a long silence. I would begin to wonder if anything was being done at all. Putting my case to the driver's insurance company was slow and laborious. We were struggling financially and hadn't paid the mortgage for months. We were having the mortgage interest paid by money received from the social services, but every so often, we would receive a letter from the bank threatening eviction if we didn't pay. We would then have to call the solicitor, who would then write to the bank on our behalf to ask for a "stay of execution". The solicitors informed the bank that I would be receiving a substantial sum of money as compensation and that any debt would then be sorted.

Most people are aware, though, that fighting insurance companies for compensation through the courts takes an incredible length of time. We had been warned that a tactic of the insurance companies is to drag it out, hoping that people give up and settle for much less than they are entitled to. I could see why. The lack of finances and all the stress it entails in fighting a case is soul-destroying. You have to be very strong to see it through. I was pig-headed and still am. Gill couldn't do anymore. She'd had enough. I have never blamed her for the actions she took after, but it was a terrible blow for me.

It was the beginning of November and well into autumn. The kids had enjoyed Bonfire Night, and we'd had a fire in the garden. We tried, where we could, to provide the kids with some normal family times so that when they looked back at their childhoods, they would hold good memories, too. Not just ones of going without. Sometimes, Gill would drive us to the forest park a few miles away so they could play cricket and run through the woods. There were some fun times. I don't think they noticed the emotional distance between their mum and dad.

Gill had come into the living room, and I noticed her eyes looked puffy and sore. She looked so terribly sad. I couldn't stand it any longer. I had to accept that there was something very wrong, and I couldn't continue burying my head in the sand any longer. I decided it was the time to give her a lead-in.

"Is there something you want to tell me, Gill?" I said.

That was all it needed.

Her face crumpled, and the floodgates opened. Her voice was quaking, but she managed to say, "Yes. Yes, there is. I've been wanting to tell you, but there has never been a good time."

She managed to get it all out, then sank back into the settee cushion and sobbed. Out came the words along the lines of she didn't mean it to happen. It just happened, etc., etc.

"Need I ask who it is? I have a good idea, but I want you to tell me." And tell me she did.

"It's Ugly Paul," she said.

Now, any other time, that reply would have been quite funny. I had been thrown into touch to make way for Ugly Paul. What an insult. Not only had I lost my wife to another man, but to a man called Ugly Paul to boot. It doesn't do a lot for the self-esteem. Even though I knew I was going to have to face this sooner or later, it still was devastating to hear her say that she didn't love me anymore. She said that I had changed so much I wasn't the man she had married, and above all, the biggest body blow: she still loved me, but like a brother. That really was the turning of the screw. She wanted to be with Paul and start a new life with him.

At that moment, what great timing: a neighbour had decided to pay us a social visit. I still feel sorry for him to this day when I think about what I put him through when I forced him to witness the domestic upset he had landed himself in. He knocked at the door, but Gill had seen him walking up the drive.

"It's Mick Smith," she said. "Don't let him come in."

I had other ideas. I opened the door and greeted him with a "hi". I asked him to come in and told him to sit down.

He asked us if we were ok, and I replied honestly.

"No, I'm afraid not. Gill has just told me she's leaving me."

After he had cast a worried glance at my face, he realised I wasn't joking and jumped up to leave. "I'm so sorry. I didn't mean to intrude. I'll, err, get out of your way," he stuttered.

"No. No," I said. "I want you to stay."

He was edging towards the door, but I insisted.

"I really do want you to stay," I said.

He tried a few more times to extricate himself from the living room, but I was having none of it. Gill scuttled into the kitchen and put the kettle on. It was quite a surreal moment. Gill asked how many sugars, and Mick asked what we were going to do. I told him it seemed out of my hands and that we hadn't discussed the finer details.

"How can you keep so cool, Dan?" he asked.

I didn't know. After all, how are you supposed to react when your wife drops a bombshell like that? Gill kept a low profile but brought Mick his cup and was doing the good hostess bit. Though it was really obvious by looking at her face that she was finding it difficult to hold it together, she went through the motions.

We exchanged our goodbyes on the doorstep, and then Mick left, after finishing with a bewildered, "I'm so sorry, mate. If there is anything I can do, let me know."

I then thanked him, and I bet he couldn't get back to his front door quickly enough.

"What did you want to do that for?" she said.

Why not? I thought, as I hadn't got anything to hide or to be ashamed of. Everyone was going to know sooner or later, and I suppose part of me wanted her to feel uncomfortable. She had decided to do this, and therefore, she should take some of the flack.

We had a lot of things to discuss and sort out. I told her I would leave the house and let her and the kids stop there. I would go to my mum's. That idea was not at all acceptable to her. She and Ugly Paul wanted to make a fresh start away from everyone around here in a new home together. My thought was that if she stayed at the family home, it would be less disruptive for the kids, as they would still be near their friends and school. However, she was adamant that they would all move and live elsewhere—in rented accommodation at first, and then they would get something more permanent in time. As a couple, they had obviously discussed this.

Gill said she didn't want to make my life any more difficult than it was, but she couldn't carry on as we had been doing. She wanted more. She didn't specify what "more" was, but I gathered it to mean more excitement, more prospects, more money and more sex, or at least some sex. I started to struggle as I began mentally to come to terms with what she was telling me. We both realised, apart from the emotional upheaval we were having to come to terms with, I was also going to be physically struggling. I was able to walk short distances at this time, but I wasn't great. Household chores were going to be difficult for me. To discuss such things seemed so cold, but Gill offered to come back to do my ironing and any other chores I couldn't cope with. What had it come to? Not only was my wife leaving me, but she pitied me enough to offer to help me out in the house afterwards. How marvellous!

At weekends, I would have the children, and she would have them during the week. As I had worked so hard through the years, she said I should keep the house. Furniture ownership didn't take a lot of sorting as we hadn't got much anyway—only the basic bare essentials.

The job of telling the kids she wanted to leave me wasn't up to me, and I wouldn't do it. If she was doing the dirty deed, then she should be the one to tell them.

After school ended for the day, the kids were going to be in for one hell of a shock: news that would have a bearing on the rest of their lives. Poor kids. They cried, and they pleaded with her, but to no avail. She had made up her mind, and they would just have to get used to it. Ugly Paul hadn't broken the news to his young wife at the time; therefore, Gill couldn't leave straight away. As I had forced the issue with Gill, I received the news before they had planned it to happen. Paul also had the extra complication of having to leave his baby daughter, who was only a few months old. Not an easy task.

Eventually, the news of the affair was broken to his wife, and it did not go well. Kate, his wife, was not the type of person to take something like that lying down. She hit the roof!

Gill and Paul managed to rent a house in town. The kids were absolutely miserable. They had moved to a strange house and had a strange, stand-in dad. School remained the same, and Gill did a longer school run, having to travel a few miles more. Fortunately for the couple, Paul's mum had a bit of money. She could lend them some for the deposit on a new-build house in the next village, but it was going to be a while before it was completed.

The kids came back to me at the weekends, and with my mum's help, I was managing to cope physically, but I felt a wreck emotionally. Gill did come from time to time and did some ironing. She wanted to show me how to use the household appliances, but I had already studied the user instruction manuals and knew what to do. I wasn't totally incapable. I missed my old life, though. I missed the kids, and I missed Gill. We had been married for 13 years, and it was odd not to have her at home.

One day, I even put a ridiculous proposition to her. I'm ashamed to even admit to it now, but I asked her if she would stay, even if it meant she had to carry on seeing Paul. Everything would go back to how it was, and I would turn a blind eye to her affair. It would be something I would have to suffer and live with. I would get some part of Gill back, and the kids would come home. Madness, I know, but it seemed a feasible idea at the time. Of course, it was rejected. She and Paul were in love and wanted to live together. When my emotions had stabilised more, I realised what a ludicrous idea it was. I bet she really pitied me then. It was the plea of a desperate man. Gill wasn't coming back, and I just had to learn to get used to it.

Gill took the car because, for one, the kids needed to get to school, and for another, I couldn't drive anyway. Five hundred pounds was also required for the bond on their rented house, and I agreed to her taking it out of our loan account. The kids needed to be settled, after all, and I couldn't deny them the chance of a home being provided for them. I could just about walk to the local shop if I took my time. I shopped at the local supermarket by walking there but stopping on the way through the park and having 'five' on the park bench to gather myself before proceeding with the rest of the journey. I would then pick up my shopping and get a taxi back home.

Weekends were taken up by playing board games with the children and generally trying to make the time with them as fun as possible. Mum would come down and help and enjoy time with them, too. The two girls shared a single bed. Gill had taken the other bed, which was part of the bunk bed, to use at their home. I moved to the main bedroom again, and Chris got his bedroom back. Routine was the key to getting through this time and coping.

After a few weeks, I stopped panicking as much and settled down. At least having the children around took my mind off any deeper issues of missing my wife, financial difficulties, and court cases. Without the kids, I would have had no reason to carry on. Some days were better than others. I began to get physically stronger, and that, in turn, gave me more strength to carry on.

Although enjoyable, weekends were upsetting when the time came for the children to return home. Gill would arrive in the car, and then the tears would start, especially from Gemma. They didn't want to go back with her; they wanted to stay. They would all cry, and I would tell them they had to go with their mum.

Things at home weren't that good, by all accounts. Gill was stressed a lot of the time. They were waiting for a new home, Gill was doing shift work at a factory, and Kate was giving Paul a hard time. It resulted in Gill getting frustrated with the kids for not doing as they were told. The kids were rebelling against being put into a situation they didn't want and were being extremely unruly. Gill was losing her patience with them quite often and had started shouting and bellowing at them. Gemma had the knack of really winding her up, something she had always had the art of doing, but it was happening more and more under these circumstances. The kids asked if they could stop with me. I explained to them that it would be much better for them to stay with their mum. Children should be with their mum, and she was much more able financially and physically to cater to their needs. Every weekend that passed, it got more and more difficult to see them off back home.

After a particular emotional departure and me again saying no to their request to stay with me, I did tell them that I couldn't ask Gill for them to stay with me permanently, as I knew she would believe that I had planned it somehow.

They needed to explain to their mum, themselves, why they were unhappy.

The following weekend, Gill wanted a word with me. She came into the living room, looking upset, and all three kids were in tow. She said that the kids had been talking to her and didn't seem to want the lifestyle she was offering them and were unhappy.

"Did you ever consider that they may not have wanted to live with you?" I asked.

"Of course they do. I'm their mum," she said.

"Well, have you ever asked them what they want?" was my response.

"No," she said, "but I just know."

"Well, ask them then," I said.

The replies she received from them weren't at all what she expected, and she looked shocked. Gemma was the first one she asked. Gemma had always been a bit of a Daddy's girl, and therefore, it was not too big of a surprise to me when she stated quite boldly that she wanted to stay with me. Gill turned to Rachel and asked her what she wanted to do. Rachel seemed a bit uncertain and hesitated a little, but Gemma had always been the leader, and Rachel usually followed suit. There was no exception this time, either. She also said she wanted to stay with me.

Gill was looking quite dejected at this stage and then turned to Chris. Being the youngest and her 'little boy',

Gill and I both expected him to say that he wanted to stay with his mum. We were both astounded when he stated he wanted to stay with me, too. It was all too much for Gill, and she left in floods of tears, having to live with the fact that all three of her children had chosen not to leave with her and had decided they were going to live with me. I didn't feel like gloating or that I'd got one up on her in any way. My prime aim was to help communicate to Gill what they really wanted. I was even shocked and then realised I would now have yet more responsibility. It was going to be a tough ride. I had a lot of learning to do, but I was going to have to do it as we went along. My physical health wasn't great. I had virtually no finances, and now I had children aged 8, 9 and 11 to look after. I was entering yet another new chapter of my life. That of a single dad.

CHAPTER 9

SINGLE DAD

How difficult could it be to get three kids up, washed, dressed, fed and to school? Well! Very difficult, as it turned out. No day was the same, and there never was a textbook type of day. Tights had got a hole in them. They couldn't find their trainers for sports or hadn't done their homework, so it had to be completed in 10 minutes, which would mean something like breakfast or tooth brushing would have to go by the wayside. There would be acute stomach pains to contend with, lost gym shirts, football boots still encased in mud from the week before that had to be cleaned, etc., etc. Every day, I would promise myself that the following day would be more organised, but no matter how much preparation was put in, there was always something I'd not accounted for. From 7.30 to 8.30 am was one almighty stressful hour.

At 8.30, regardless, we would have to set off on foot across the bridle path towards the small church school. Leaving at that time meant we would be five minutes late, but that was acceptable, albeit irksome, for the headteacher. However, the children could still slip into the main hall for morning assembly without causing too much disruption.

Very often, the neighbour's children would tag along. The working mums would be grateful as they could get off to work in their cars knowing that the kids were in safe hands, which gave them a bit of a breather and a quieter start to their morning. As I would have to walk the path anyway, another three or four kids wouldn't make any difference.

When the weather was good, it was quite a nice walk through the meadows, passing the elderberry bushes and flowery meadowsweet. Single file because of the patches of nettles on the way. Past the old railway carriage, which was used for the old Shire horse that had been grazing in the pasture for years. A couple of the younger kids would always be wary, even though I doubted if the old mare was in any way dangerous. Nevertheless, when you are only six or seven years old, the sight of a big bay horse with a shaggy mane and tail heading towards you can be quite intimidating. A quick look behind would then be in order to check that all kids had passed the carriage. Sometimes, carrots would have to be used as a decoy, and then onwards, over the stone flags and the little footbridge. Another quick check then to give a little prompt to Chris and the boys not to stop on the bridge to spit in the brook. It was then up the Roman cobbled bridle path, coming out at the top near the bench. Next, we were on the main road, where I would have to be more vigilant with looking over the kids because of the traffic, gathering them all together for the last 200 yards of tarmac pavement. Then, at last, in through the school gates. The Pied Piper's work was then done. Jobs a good 'un.

A big outward breath and then head back home at a more leisurely pace. Depending on how I was feeling, I would sometimes have a brief pit stop at the bench to recuperate. What a relief it would be to rest my knees and ankles. Legs sprawled out and face lifted to the sun with eyes closed, drinking in the warmth and knowing I'd got a good few hours before I needed to pick up the pace for their return. Love the kids as I did, 10 minutes of peace in the sunshine, looking at the meadows and watching blackbirds, thrushes and robins in and out of the hedgerows and undergrowth was a delight.

Sometimes, a flock of geese in formation would go past, heading towards the ponds nearby. This was the place where the old pit had been, and I would sometimes find myself reminiscing about my working days. I remember looking at the winding gear, standing like a monument on the landscape. A wheel mounted on top of a tower of crisscrossed metal. To some people, it would probably have been considered a blot, but to me and most of my friends, it was a part of our everyday environment. We thought it would stand forevermore and was a sign that there would always be jobs in the pit for our sons and our son's sons. But that had all gone now, and man-made ponds added to the landscape. Fishing platforms jutted out from the sides of the ponds, and the surrounding area was all planted with trees.

Little did I know when I was a young apprentice walking past, towards the drift mine where I worked, that Maggie Thatcher would shut down near on all the pits at this stage. Three pits had gone in close succession, and the few big ones that were still open were private. Anyone wanting a job at one of those meant they had to travel quite a distance, and there would be so many men after too few jobs. Who would have thought it? And in my lifetime, too. No more slag heaps. They had now been flattened to form a new plantation of willows. The winding gear had been removed, and the wheel that stuck out proudly into the sky was now just an ornament to mark the entrance to the newly formed 'country park'. It was progress, I guess, but it had been so hard for the community to adjust, especially as the jobs had gone before the new ones had been created. To be honest, though, I didn't really want my son to join me down the black hole to dig out some of the black stuff. I just hoped that there would be something else there for him. Unfortunately, though, this was a time of transition, so men were still trying to get retrained and travelling to other places for work. I, too, had to move around pits travelling further afield in order to stay in work. Well, maybe my kids would work hard at school and be high achievers. I really hoped so, especially as they hadn't had a lot of luck thrown their way at this stage. Mum's gone off with a man, and Dad's a cripple. Great stuff! *It can only get better, kids.*

Because my physical health improved very slowly, I didn't really notice and felt I was not progressing at all. In the evening, I would sometimes reflect on the day, and I could get really morose, especially if it had been a bad day. I still tired easily through the day, and I was still in quite a lot of pain. My back still had muscle spasms. My wrists were so fragile that I could hardly carry any weight in my hands, and I had terrible headaches amongst the general aches and pains over my body.

Night-times were always the worst. I could frighten myself with worry over what the future held for my children and for me. Was I doing enough? Would they be better with Gill? What if I felt too bad to cope with them? Was I wise taking them on if I then had to send them to their mum's if I couldn't manage? The mornings sat on the bench in the sun, reminiscing over my past seemed so much more enjoyable than the nights, full of worry about what might be lying ahead for us all.

As my days were so full of the chores I needed to do to keep our household ticking over, they passed quite quickly. All the day-to-day duties that most people take in their stride had to be strategically planned. My weekly shopping was done at the local supermarket. To keep within my budget, this involved walking to the supermarket in two stages. I would walk through St George's Park and stop to rest on one of the park benches in the Peace Garden to give my knees a break. After having 'five', I would then carry on to the supermarket.

The shopping list would have been constructed throughout the week but didn't deviate very much from one list to the next. I got to know what the kids liked and would eat, and therefore, I stuck to what worked. As I had a poor memory because of the accident, I used to keep the list in the kitchen, and I added items to it each day. Very often, the list would have 'extra' items on, in child's scrawl: Mars Bars, Twix biscuits, sherbet fountains, pink fluffy biscuits with coconut on. There would be no question as to who would add 'Spray hair gel - NOT CHEAP STUFF IN A JAR'. That would be Gemma. She would also try to add 'mascara-black, cheap one will do'. At 12 years old, I don't think so. The hair gel she would get. She assured me it was a necessity for every 12-year-old girl. I didn't know if it was or wasn't, so I had to concede that point and give her the benefit of the doubt. The mascara, now that was easier for me to deal with, and I was able to say a definite no.

As I knew the prices of the usual weekly stuff, I soon learnt to budget quite well. But if I had the gas bill due, then the weekly shop had to be reduced. It was a fine art juggling the bills, but I managed. Every week, I would ensure that the kids had a bag of sweets each. It was up to them how quickly they chose to eat them, but there would be no more until the following Thursday. I gathered up the washing each day and placed it in the washing machine. The timer was set each evening to take advantage of the cheaper electricity rates. The dishwasher was also set up to operate through the night.

Mum would visit and give me a helping hand with tidying the kid's bedrooms and emptying bins. I still had to fit in numerous hospital appointments.

The weeks passed, and we were still all intact, so I was managing. My cousin, Paul, would visit me most evenings when the kids were in bed, and we would have a few games of pool. I had a small pool table in the garage, and the hour or so we spent in there at night helped take my mind off things and gave me a little relief from my chores of the day. Sometimes, my other friends would pop around and we would all play together. It was awkward holding and positioning the cue, but I adapted. We got quite silly, but as they say, "Once a boy, always a boy". It was all good fun. We had aliases when we played, like "Bang on Billy Johnny", which was my friend John Maiden, and Cousin Paul was "Whirlwind Worth". We would do our own commentary, and very often we couldn't play because we were laughing so much. I don't think they realised how much it meant to me back then. Paul's wife, Kim, and my cousin Barbara would cook for me, plate the meals up, and bring them down. They spoilt me, and it was good to know that people cared.

I was told by a neighbour only recently that, at the time, she used to watch me limping up the road to return over an hour later with a loaf from the local shop. She knew what a feat it was for me to do, and yet, for someone else, it would only be a fifteen-minute journey. She said she would look at me and think, *Poor bugger! On his own, looking after those kids, and he can barely walk.* She did say that she was so surprised after a few months to find I was coping ok and still managing to hold it all together. Gill didn't show her face around much then, except for picking the kids up and dropping them off.

Gemma didn't want to go and visit her mum that often as she had her friends around the corner. They had a pony, so she spent a lot of time there, helping with the mucking out and grooming. I, however, was aware she would need her mum during the teenage years, which were fast approaching. Or maybe it was me who would need her to have her mum around her. I wasn't too sure if I had all the attributes needed for giving emotional support to teenage daughters. Very often, I would have to act as a mediator between Gill and Gemma, as they could be so volatile when they got together. Sometimes, this involved me having to take Gemma back early from Gill's or Gemma having a weekend off while things cooled down.

The necessity of doing the everyday things kept me physically and mentally occupied for most of the day. I didn't have much time to think about my personal needs and what my long-term prognosis for my own recovery would be. I still had very dark phases when I had to push the images of young Matt out of my mind. I wondered if I would ever return to work.

I hadn't thought much about the prospect of ever meeting anyone else or having a relationship with another woman. All attempts early on in my recovery had proved fruitless when seeking any improvement on the sexual response side. Even now, I find it difficult to actually call it what it is. I was impotent. If I didn't have to encounter it, then I wouldn't have to tag myself with that kind of label. I would just choose not to meet anyone. That way, it would possibly mean I was too busy to take a partner on board, and at worst, it would make me a lonely single dad, but it would not make me impotent. I would just be a victim of circumstance. Financially, I had nothing to offer. I had no job, no prospects, three kids, a serious limp, a bad back, and a mortgage I had no chance of paying. Hell! Impotence didn't even come into it. I had a list as long as your arm that would be enough to put off any prospective admirer. She'd have to be desperate, blind and mentally challenged and maybe all three to take me on. I had made up my mind to be a lonely, single dad.

CHAPTER 10

BACK IN THE REAL WORLD

I was beginning to get a handle on things now. My life settled into a routine. I was at a bit of a loose end when the kids were at their mum's at the weekend, especially when I didn't get a visit from my friends. They had been trying to convince me that I should step out into the real adult world and start to go out in the evening on my own. I wasn't sure about that. I still needed to have a toilet close by. Although much improved, I still had bladder problems. It was what the doctors called an "urgency" problem, which meant that I didn't get much notice before I needed to pee. I therefore had to be careful what trousers I wore. They had to be quick release. My fingers were crossed over and rotated on my right hand, and unbuttoning anything was awkward, so zips were the only option. I learnt this the hard way.

Anthony and John would take me for a drink every so often. It was only to the local pub, and everyone knew me. In fact, it was surprising I ever went with Anthony at all, especially after one of the first outings we had together. He convinced me to have the extra pint, even though my instinct told me not to. I had it anyway; I am so easily led astray. I drank the pint, but then I needed to go to the loo and quickly. I got up, trying to look as cool as possible and tried to make it as fast as I could to the men's. I just managed to hobble there, and then I realised not soon enough that I had put on my beige chinos, which were button flies. My fingers plaited their way along my buttons, but I was too late. The floodgates opened, and there it was, a big wet patch in front of my beige trousers. I could have cried. I didn't know what to do.

Anthony came in to find me, and then, when he saw what a state I was in, he decided to make light relief of it, so to speak, and laughed out loud.

"It's alright for you," I said, "but what am I going to do now?"

He had a plan. I was to follow him closely, and then he would hide my embarrassment with his own body. At 20 stone, it was big enough. I would then get back to the table and slide my body back under the table onto my chair. I had no other choice but to try it.

All went well until we got almost to our table. There were still another couple of friends sitting there also, and to my horror, Anthony jumped to the side.

"Look what he's done!" he shouted.

I wanted the floor to swallow me, and I would have liked something large and vicious to swallow Anthony, preferably bit by bit, with as much pain as possible involved.

My friends rolled in laughter, and I had a few comments while they enjoyed my predicament.

"I'll kill you, Ant!" I said.

But he just said, "We all know now, mate. No need to try and hide it. Worry over! Who cares anyway?"

Next time, I will ask him for full plan details before I go ahead. Still, like all good stories, there was a moral. Don't wear light-coloured button-fly trousers. Don't have that extra pint. And whatever you do, don't listen to friends' advice.

I'm always a pushover when friends are involved; however, I do value them enormously. So, when the lads were on and on about me going out to town and having a laugh with them, they wore me down enough for me to agree.

So one Friday night, when the kids were with Gill, I put on my best black zipped trousers and my newest shirt and went to town on the bus. I met a couple of my friends and, with my limited budget, we frequented three or four pubs in the town centre. I had a great time and saw lots of old mates from the pit and old acquaintances from my days on the doors. Faces from 15 years before when, as a young apprentice, going to town on a Friday night was a regular thing. Not a lot had changed, really, except we were all older and carried a few more life scars. Some were divorced and going out again for their second wind at tangling and fraternising with the ladies. Some had never stopped going. Still being boys forever. I really enjoyed it, and although exhausted, I decided I would do it again when finances and health permitted.

It got to where the nights were a great release for me. I did get the odd bit of attention from the opposite sex, but I used to nip all interest in the bud. I wasn't looking too bad physically at this stage. I had managed to regulate my eating and balance my weight. Pain had been etched on my face, making me look drawn and old, but the improvement of my general health and pain relief tablets had helped. When I had bouts of bad pain, I wouldn't go out anyway. I was also using a few training weights in the garage to help try to get some condition back. I had to tape the weight bar to my hands as I couldn't make a fist, and it was very painful, but I wanted to do as much as I could to help with my recovery. No pain, no gain. I was improving all the time, but at this stage, it had been over a year since the accident.

I was still seeing doctors and solicitors, and it was still slow going. I had also started to go with Ian Cummins, Matt's brother, to motocross on a Sunday. He would pick me up in the van, and I would watch him compete in the motocross races. Sometimes, I would be so exhausted when we had done that I would have to lie full length in the van on the way back. It was a silly thing to do, really, as at night, my back would spasm and I'd be in agony, but I enjoyed the company. Also, I can't thank him enough for the emotional help it gave me in knowing he didn't blame me and he was able to laugh and joke with me and treat me like a mate. I don't know if he realised how much that helped me, and Emma, his wife, was just so supportive, too. Bless them both.

Gradually, without even realising, my life was getting better, and less painful than it had been. I started to get used to being on my own and having the single dad's life. I devoted the weekdays to my children and had a kind of single life evolving around my mates and bikes at the weekend. I still didn't look long term at things.

CHAPTER 11

MEETING THE GIRL

It was a Friday night, and I was all spruced up with my black trousers and my signature aftershave. I still use the same aftershave now. It's by Ralph Lauren, and I'm often given compliments on how good I smell, so why change it? I'd been going to town for four or five months, about every three weeks or so. I couldn't afford to go more often. The pubs in town were lively, and most played good music. It was a great atmosphere. I would finish off with a takeaway snack, then catch the last bus home. I had some good times. I chatted with the ladies, but was careful not to encourage them too much.

My life carried on in this vein for a while: looking after the kids all week, and when I could afford to, donning my best outfit and hitting the town on a Friday night where I could forget my worries and have a laugh with my mates whilst drinking a few Buds. [Budweiser]

One particular warm and barmy Friday night, three of us were having a night on the town. It was busy as there were lots of people around the pubs due to the warm weather. Girls, in their summer tops and strappy sandals and suntanned chaps with their bottles of beer, were standing outside in the forecourts of the pubs. All were laughing and joking and all in a good mood, looking forward to the weekend and enjoying the sun. My friend John and I were just about to enter one of the high street pubs, and I noticed one of the girls standing outside. Tina was the sister of a mate I'd been to technical college with. I'd not seen her for years, but she seemed to recognise me, and when I gave her a second look, I realised it was Tina. She was about 12 years old when I used to go to her house with her brother, Pete.

"Hi," she said. "Do you remember me?"

"Of course I remember you. It's little Tina."

She was only slightly built, so little Tina was still an apt name for her. We exchanged pleasantries, and I asked her what she was doing hanging around outside. She was waiting for her friend to arrive, and although the bus she was due to arrive on had already been and gone, she felt sure she was still going to turn up. She knew she'd be late but would turn up eventually. Sure enough, a couple of minutes later, a taxi pulled up, and a woman got out. She was apologising as she came hurrying towards us with a brolly in her hands and a jacket over her arm.

"Sorry! I missed the bus, and it took me a while to get a taxi."

She looked all harassed but had a lovely, warm smile, and I smiled back. It was quite clear that she was not used to going around town. You don't bother with coats as the pubs are always busy and crowded and you never bring a brolly. I was quite amused by the sight of her. I did notice, however, that she'd got a pretty face, lovely long, wavy chestnut hair, and she looked very friendly, albeit her looking slightly out of place. Tina introduced us. I soon learnt that her name was Karen and that it was her first night on the town. She had moved house that day, and although she wasn't expecting to, Tina had convinced her that an evening out would be a release from her worries. Karen was Tina's work colleague, who had recently separated from her husband and was setting up in a new home with her two children.

Although she had to be persuaded by her colleagues to have a night out as she had been going through a rough time, splitting up from her husband hadn't been easy. Karen said she had no idea what to wear, as she had thought herself out of the fashion scene. She'd been married for 16 years and wasn't quite sure what was considered cool anymore. I told her she looked great and that no one would have guessed. I lied. She would have to ditch the brolly and coat in the future, but nevertheless, I did find her attractive and, most of all, she had a very sweet personality. We talked for a few more minutes and said that we would probably bump into each other later. We did – a few times.

I always find it uncanny how groups of people doing the town's pubs seem to follow a similar trail. There's the 'in' pubs and the ones that go temporarily out of fashion. Then, for some strange reason, they are part of the pub trail again. It can't be explained, but it happens, so there was a high probability that around the 12 or so pubs we were certainly going to bump into each other again. We did, and each time, we would have a bit of a chat and a laugh.

A couple of weeks later, I did the town pub run again with mates, and we bumped into each other again. She looked much more like a seasoned towngoer by then. Her clothes were fresh from a fashion clothes shop, and she had ditched the uncool accessories. She wasn't small, but she had a nice curvy figure. Although she wore makeup, it wasn't overdone like some of the girls, so she came across as being natural-looking. When she smiled, which she did often, she lit up the place. I was getting to like her. Although she was certainly easy on the eye, it was her friendly, open personality that I found so attractive. I thought she had great potential for being a good friend. I couldn't even consider anything else, and I kidded myself that maybe I could allow her into my life as just that and not expect to take the relationship any further. She was the only girl that I even considered the possibility of perhaps building some kind of relationship with. Platonic level only, of course, and I know she seemed to like my company too. It got that when I went to town, I was actually hoping I would bump into her. My friend John went along with my thoughts and believed Karen was such a nice girl that there would be no reason we couldn't be friends. Not only was I kidding myself, but I also had John to back me.

As the weeks passed, Karen and I got to know each other more and more. Sometimes, it would be up to three weeks before we would see each other again. We learnt quite a lot about each other. It was good to be able to talk with someone and have them understand what problems being a lone parent brought. We chatted about all kinds of subjects. She was also funny and witty, and we seemed to be on the same spiritual plane.

Then, the inevitable happened. I started to imagine: *What if?* What if I could have a relationship one step up from a friendship? Maybe we could hold and kiss each other, and maybe then I could tell her about my injuries and what happened to me. Maybe, just maybe, she would understand and say it was ok—that it didn't matter that I wasn't what you call a "complete man".

We had shared so much over the months I had known her. She was very understanding, and she might be ok with not having a complete physical relationship. What was I thinking? I couldn't go there. At best, it would frighten her off, and at worst, she may think of me as a freak. Maybe someone to feel sorry for or even laugh at. No, I couldn't confide in her. That was a bad plan. Yet I was finding myself thinking more and more about *What if?* From initially enjoying the relationship, it was now growing more complicated. I knew that to be sure I wasn't going to get hurt, I would have to end it while I could.

I met her the next Friday night, and although I intended to finish the friendship with some kind of excuse, I found I couldn't. I knew I would miss her too much and decided to enjoy her company a bit longer. Instead of making the excuse, I asked her if she wanted to go to a nightclub with me. I still had some friends who worked on the doors at the clubs in town, so the chances were I could get us free entrance into one. She agreed straight away, and we linked arms as we walked to the club.

I then did a showing-off thing. Not really like me at all, but we were both slightly drunk, and I was enjoying Karen's companionship, especially as it was an evening with her I didn't expect. I walked to the front of the queue and saw it was Russ on the door.

"Is it ok, Russ, if I bring a friend in with me?"

"Sure," he said and stepped back to let us through.

A few of the people around groaned as we jumped the queue. I thought in a boyish way that Karen might have been impressed. I was being a real prat: like a 16-year-old boy in love and showing off to his girl. We had a great evening, however. We huddled up close. We danced—in a fashion where I was concerned, but at least I had always had a sense of rhythm, so I could sway in time with the best of them. We both drank lots of bottles of beer, and giggled and danced together until the early hours. I almost forgot about my "shortcomings". With Karen, I felt normal.

There had been a bit of a ruckus due to some drunk getting slightly hot-headed and causing trouble. Russ went in to ask him to leave. The drunk refused and went for Russ's blind side. I jumped up and quickly grabbed him in an arm-locked. I then passed him on to Russ, who led him through the door. Russ thanked me as he escorted the drunk out. A little of the old Dan Church had returned.

Karen and I left the nightclub. She thanked me for the good evening, and I said she would be going home. I told her I would walk her to the taxi rank, but she told me she would walk home. She said it wasn't far, and that she refused to pay the extra charge for a cab as it was after midnight, so fares would be double. I didn't like the idea of her going home alone. I wasn't sure if I could walk a long distance as I had already been on my feet a while and was struggling, but she had said it wasn't far. After the good night, I decided to take a chance and offered to walk her home. I had also had quite a lot of alcoholic anaesthetic, and so at 2 o'clock in the morning, we linked arms and headed for her home.

The walk was gruelling, and I finished up walking much further than I'd ever walked after the accident. So much for her saying it was only a short distance. My back was throbbing, and my knees were grinding. The effects of the drink had started to wear off, and I was beginning to panic. My God! What was I doing? It had seemed a good idea at the time, but I was wondering if I could even make the walk back to her place, and what would I do then anyway?

Eventually, we arrived at her house, and we both went inside. It was a modern, comfortable home with photographs of her children on the mantelpiece. We had already discussed each other's family. Her two children were staying at her mother's for the night, so there was only us in the house. She continued to chat away, and we had a coffee. I had no idea what I was going to do to get back. I was about 10 miles from home and it was just before four in the morning. I would not be able to get a bus, but I doubted I could walk another step. Karen also seemed to be winding down. We were both very tired, and she offered me the spare room for the night. All of a sudden, she said she was going to bed and headed off up the stairs. She said she'd see me in the morning and said goodnight with a yawn.

I made my way upstairs and called her name, as I wanted to make sure I was going to the right room.

I opened the door into what turned out to be her room, and she was already curled up under the duvet, fast asleep. I went into one of the other bedrooms. It looked like her little boy's room. I took off my shirt and trousers and lay on the bed.

Day was breaking, and I didn't feel at all comfortable. I had done something really foolish. In the cold light of day, I was in a different frame of mind. What was I thinking, playing at happy couples? I couldn't see this through. If I let her in too much, she would be sure to find out. At that moment, I could perhaps get away with seeming to be doing the gentlemanly thing and not being too pushy with her, but I wouldn't be able to keep that up forever. At some point, she was going to expect more, and she would be really disappointed when it wasn't ever going to happen.

I'd been a fool to think I could carry on with this relationship, but for a few hours, I had forgotten I was only part of a man. I had chatted, giggled, danced and fraternised with a lovely, pretty lady who seemed to really enjoy my company, too. However, it was time to call it a day. I'd been mulling the thoughts over and over again. A tear welled in my eye and slowly began to trickle down my cheek. I then took a deep intake of breath and sat on the edge of the bed. I put on my trousers and shirt and walked out onto the landing. I could hear Karen breathing heavily in her room. It was obvious she was still asleep.

I tiptoed downstairs. I put on my jacket, and at the front door, I found my shoes where I had left them a couple of hours before and put them on. At least I had rested my poor, aching feet; they were now feeling a lot better than they had been.

I decided to walk off the estate and to the main road, where I would then be able to catch a bus to town and then, from town, catch another bus home. I must have looked like something the cat had dragged in. I was still limping, and I hadn't had a wink of sleep all night.

After another hour or so, I managed to get back myself home. My kids were still at their mum's, so I went straight to the bedroom, got into bed and slept.

The next morning, I awoke late. I was aching all over. I had made up my mind that I wouldn't see Karen anymore. Not on a date, anyway. I would just say hello and keep her at arm's length. Although I had got her telephone number as we had already said we would go on a proper date with each other, I wasn't going to call her, and I threw away her number so I wouldn't be tempted. I would miss her. It made me feel lonely thinking about it, but I really didn't think I had a choice.

I went back to my usual routine. I didn't realise that, in the meantime, Karen had remembered that one of my friends had mentioned that I lived in Staveley with a train track at the bottom of the garden. He also mentioned I lived near a scrap merchant. She already knew that I lived in a bungalow and it was near to the school. She then decided to try to find me.

One Sunday afternoon, I was seeing my friend out to his car. He had been an old work colleague who had called in for a coffee to see how I was doing. It was while I was standing at the top of my drive that I saw Karen at the bottom of it. I clocked her, and she looked embarrassed. It was good to see her, though. I beckoned her up and introduced her to my friend Robbie. He smiled and then got in his car. I asked her where her car was, and she mumbled something about it being at the top of the road. I told her to bring the car down onto the drive while I put the kettle on. I was looking forward to chatting with her. I had missed her.

We talked for ages. She explained that when she awoke that morning after I had been to her home, she was surprised that I wasn't still there. She felt really guilty because she had been completely overcome by tiredness and crashed out. She realised I must have had to get myself home, and she had felt terrible about it. When I hadn't called, she thought I had been offended by something she had done, and therefore, she had tried to find me to apologise. After reassuring her she had nothing to apologise for, we chatted over a few coffees for a couple of hours. It was like relaxing with an old friend. It felt so right, and she looked as beautiful as ever. I wasn't going to give her up just yet. I enjoyed her company too much.

Over the next few weeks, I met her at lunchtime at work. We would go into a little café up a side street from the town centre, and it would be wrong to say we chatted. *She* chatted, and I listened. An hour was all the time she could have. I'd meet her outside, and I would see her walking briskly up towards me. Karen worked in an office and always looked well turned out, in fitted skirts and co-ordinating shoes and a long wool coat. Her face would break out in a smile as she saw me. Her choice of lipstick was usually a toned-down red, and with her dark colouring, it really suited her. Her coat would flap around her body as she never buttoned it and was always in a rush.

After a swift hello and a peck on the cheek, we would go and sit at our usual table, and the waiter would take our order. Two coffees and either jacket potatoes and salad or two small plates of spaghetti Bolognese. Karen would always have some story of something that had happened to her that day. She would throw her head back, and her dark, wavy hair would flick over her shoulders. Her laugh was infectious. I was barely able to get a word in because she was so anxious to tell her stories and had so little time. I used to joke with her and tell her to slow down.

All too soon, she would glance at her watch and say she would have to dash. In a flash, she would be gone out the door, coat swirling around her legs. Sometimes, I would walk her back to the large office block where she worked, but she was usually in too much of a rush and would have to run down the road to get back in time. I wouldn't have been able to keep up. Karen was like a ray of sunshine who whirled into my life for an hour and ran back out again, leaving behind a smile on my face and a warm glow in my chest. It would take two bus rides to meet her for less than an hour, but it was worth it. I didn't know how I would give her up when the time came, but I decided not to think about it.

Some Sundays, Karen would call in for coffee. It was easier for her, as she had a car. We also had the odd night out around town on a Friday. She always looked great, and I always looked forward to seeing her. It seemed that a particular song would follow us around wherever we went. This seems to happen to a lot of people. The song becomes 'their' song. Ours was "You Are My Destiny" by Lionel Ritchie. We heard it hundreds of times. It always made us smile and still does.

However, I continued to have deep, depressive times that would descend suddenly. I didn't think I deserved to be happy. I thought about Matt every day, and I felt guilty that I was experiencing happiness again when he would never be able to. I still had lots of physical pain, and it was an ongoing battle with the legal case. Although ok in themselves, the kids were struggling emotionally with the split. Financially, I was struggling to make ends meet. My emotional state swung erratically from happiness, followed by guilt and depression. I didn't deserve to be alive and happy, and I knew, sooner or later, Karen would discover my terrible secret. She had already told me that she found it quite refreshing that I hadn't pushed a physical relationship onto her straight away, and it was nice to get to know each other as friends first. She had come out of a bad marriage and didn't want to feel pressured. She was glad of the steady pace. Little did she know then, but the pace wasn't going to be picked up soon or ever.

Some days, I would tell her I would ring her to make arrangements to meet, but then, if I was in a low state, I wouldn't call her. She would arrive on my doorstep all upset and ask me why I hadn't called her. Didn't I want to meet her? She knew that when we were together, we got on so well. She could sense that I thought something of her as she did me, but then I would be so standoffish with her. What I was doing was upsetting her tremendously. I was sending out mixed signals, and she didn't understand. When I wasn't with her, I could partly convince myself that I could back off and end it before we both got hurt, but when I saw her, I couldn't do it. She had become too important to me.

CHAPTER 12

COMING CLEAN

I had been feeling down and depressed, and I was still experiencing pain in my back and legs. These kinds of feelings soon spiralled out of control, and I would feel wretched. I hadn't shaved, and each day was a struggle. I hadn't seen Karen for a few days. I knew I couldn't keep my secret much longer from her. We had always talked about lots of different subjects with each other, including our pasts and our dreams for the future.

She once asked me what injuries I had received in the accident, and I just said "Multiple." I was careful about her not reading some of the statements that were written as part of my court case with the insurance company. The catalogue of injuries listed made for gruesome reading, but I specifically didn't want Karen to read the section on soft tissue injuries. Anyone reading that one testicle had been removed and that the other one was so badly damaged that only a small part remained would know that the probability of regaining the ability to have a full sex life would be practically nil.

However, the time had come to tell her. It wasn't fair for me to let her carry on like this. I had tried to end it with her, but I couldn't do it. I had spent enough time wrestling with what was the best way to approach the subject. I decided to just come clean. I would apologise for not telling her before, and I would say goodbye to her after consoling her and telling her I completely understood when she would say she couldn't see me anymore. I would then put on a brave face, and she would leave. I would then just have to get used to being alone again. I had made up my mind that this seemed to be the best option. It was actually the truth, and I felt I was well and truly in the corner now, so nothing else would do.

It was a workday for Karen, and I rang her to say that I would like her to come for a coffee at lunchtime. I'd never done this before, but she didn't question it and said she would arrive at my house at about 12.30. She knew I was feeling a little low, so maybe she thought it had something to do with that.

The morning dragged. I took a shower and put on my black jeans and a dark T-shirt. I had worn this combination before, and she had remarked how nice I looked. I had put on my usual Polo aftershave, and after glancing at the clock, I put on the kettle. I heard her car coming up the drive and saw her elegantly getting out of it. I tried to capture the image so that I could store and recall it in the future. It would probably be the last time I would see her do it.

I greeted her at the front door, not giving her a chance to ring the doorbell. She smiled as she came in and took off her coat. She had a tight, mink-coloured fitted skirt, a shell pink blouse, and black stilettos. She looked and smelled great. I gulped and thought to myself, *No going back now.*

Karen sat on the sofa. I brought the coffees in and seated myself in the chair opposite her. She looked expectantly at me, sensing that I was about to say something of importance. I took a deep breath and started the daunting task. I asked her if she knew that something had been bothering me. She answered that sometimes she thought there was something bothering me that she didn't understand, but didn't think it was too important as she knew I cared for her, so it wasn't my feelings for her that were in question. She knew the accident had caused and still was causing me a lot of stress, and she thought it was somehow connected with that.

I told her there was something important I'd got to tell her and that I was sorry I hadn't said anything before. I was dreading having to talk to her about a sensitive subject and worried like hell that if I told her, she wouldn't want to see me again. That last bit really got her attention, and she looked a little panicked.

I needed to finish this quickly. I told her I liked her a lot, but I wasn't right for her. I had three children to look after and no job prospects, plus physical disabilities that could eventually lead to further health problems when I was older. I had nothing to offer her, and I explained that as I was beginning to have feelings for her, I felt it wasn't fair to carry on seeing her. I confessed that I enjoyed her company so much that I had put off having this conversation with her.

There! I had said it. Not quite all of it, but maybe that was enough to do the trick. Karen sat very quietly. It was not like her at all. The moment seemed surreal. She didn't look remotely fazed and just said that she knew all that already, and it didn't put her off. She wanted to be with me. I had feelings of relief mixed with feelings of anxiety. Well! I was going to have to deliver the biggy. This, I was sure, was going to alter everything.

"Do you remember when you asked me what injuries I had suffered as a result of the accident? Well, I know the answer I gave you wasn't a good one. 'Multiple' wasn't an adequate answer. The fact is, I suffered injuries I should have explained earlier. Do you ever wonder why I haven't tried to make any kind of sexual advance to you?" My God, she hadn't realised how much I wanted to.

Karen still sat there very quietly and then replied softly. "It's because you are gentle and caring. You realised we'd both been hurt and needed to go at a steady pace."

I have never been loutish in my approach to women, but the answer she gave wasn't the correct one. Sweet, though, it was, and it did have some element of truth.

"Well," I said tentatively, "that's right, but there is something else. Something really big that I haven't told you." I couldn't believe how calmly the words seemed to come out of my mouth. I told her the injuries I had suffered were considerable and it would mean that I could never have a full sexual relationship or any more children. I told her I had nothing to offer her at all and that I was useless to her.

Phew! That was it. I had done it. At long last, my secret was out. I exhaled slowly. My eyes had been lowered throughout the time I had been talking. I raised them and looked at her, almost afraid to see how she would react. She looked into my eyes and placed her hand on my knee.

"Is that all the problem is?" she said. "I wondered what was bothering you. Don't worry about that. I spent the last few years of my marriage trying to avoid it. I had more than a few headaches to avoid sex with my husband. It's not the be-all and end-all of a relationship, you know. The meeting of souls is so much more important. I personally think sex is overrated. There is something much deeper to be shared between a couple than that."

I couldn't believe it. I was sure she would dash out of the door never to return, but she seemed to be saying it didn't matter. I had to be sure. "What do you mean?" I asked.

"It's not as important as you think," she said. And although she thought it would be nice if we could have sex, she was sure we could work around it and that it didn't mean we couldn't be close or sleep together. We could work it out between us, she was sure. "Don't worry about this," she said. "It's all out in the open now and we can move on."

I wanted to throw my arms around her. I was overjoyed, but something told me not to get too excited. "You might change your mind after a while and regret your decision. I won't hold you to it, you know. If you feel it is too much to bear, after all, I will understand."

Karen took both my hands in hers. She had watery eyes as she looked into mine. She told me I was the kindest, gentlest person she had known, that she liked me very much and wanted the relationship to grow between us. She gave me a little kiss on my lips and said she had to get back to work.

After putting on her coat, she looked at me and gave me a little smile. "Ring me later," she said, and then she was gone. Not like a whirling dervish this time. She walked slowly to her car and gave me a little wave before driving off. She looked beautiful. She *was* beautiful. I shed a quiet tear of relief.

I still couldn't believe my luck. Karen and I were building a relationship together. However, I still couldn't get it out of my mind that she hadn't quite realised the full implications of her response to my disclosure. Still!

It was such a relief to have it all out in the open. No more secrets. I made a private bet with myself that she would eventually realise the consequences and that she would probably leave me anyway. I gave it two years at the most.

In those early days, I know I wasn't always easy to get along with. My terrible insecurities led me to be quite moody at times. I was still having lots of pain, too, which didn't add to the smooth running of our relationship. Guilt was also a big factor in my state of mind. It was as if I needed to throw a spanner in the works if our lives were progressing too well.

There were moments when I was so happy and full of hope for my future that the guilt of it could force me into a morose state, all in the same day. It wasn't like that every day, though, and I experienced pure delight just being in her company. We watched films together. We felt a need to be close together, and to touch each other. There were no exciting day trips or candlelit dinners, as we couldn't afford it. Just being together and sharing moments were enough.

We started sharing a bed together, and I can't even remember how that began. It must have happened so naturally. We held each other close and spent hours talking, even in bed. We'd tell each other jokes and giggle. We just couldn't help relaying stories and tales until the early hours of the morning, and we would fall asleep huddled together. To feel her warm, soft body next to me was so comforting. If she found any of this difficult, she certainly didn't let it show. I knew she had come out of a difficult marriage which had been loveless for the last few years at least. She often told me how happy she was when she was with me, and it all seemed genuine. Sometimes, when she was asleep, I would have my arms wrapped around her. I could feel the quiet rhythm of her breathing and I would wonder how much time we had left.

At times, I would watch Karen dress. I would feel frustrated and long to pull her back onto the bed. I wanted to smother her with her hard kisses and show her how passionate and masculine I could be. She would catch me looking at her and be oblivious to the thoughts running through my head. She would give me one of her smiles and continue to dress. I think she would be so shocked to know what I was actually thinking. Maybe she thought if I couldn't physically do it, I wouldn't think about doing it. She would have been wrong, though. I had to be satisfied with my life now. This was as near to normal as it was going to get.

We still had the day-to-day running of our lives to contend with. Karen had her house, children and full-time job to manage, and I had my children and the constant battles and bargaining with banks and building societies to keep the wolf from my door. Karen would help me out with paying the odd bill here and there, but she had her own mortgage and bills to pay, plus child care fees too. She hadn't got much to spare, and I always told her not to worry about me, but she would help where she could, even without my approval.

I would still meet her at lunchtime sometimes, and she had started to call up one evening in the week with her children. They were a little younger than mine, so the visit would only be until about 7.30 as they would need to be bathed and put to bed. We grabbed moments where we could in the week, but the weekends were usually ours. We'd visit friends in the evening or go and look around the town shops in the day.

My health was still improving gradually, and I was able to walk longer distances. I didn't dare think about long-term plans too much. I had set a goal of two years, and this had become a milestone for me. If we were still together, then maybe we might have a chance. Luckily, Karen had kept some of her thoughts on our relationship to herself. This was just as well at the time because I would have been even more cynical about our relationship lasting.

She told me years later that, on that day when I told her that there was no chance of a sexual relationship between us, it had caused her great inner turmoil. She had driven back to work after the meeting at my house. She had given me all the right answers, as far as I was concerned.

However, as she was driving back to the office, she became quite emotional. She had wondered if she had done the right thing in the spur of the moment. Holding my hands, she had reassured me I had nothing to worry about and that a full sexual relationship wasn't the be-all and end-all. Yet when she drove away, she was crying and really wondered if she could deal with it. She said she had spent the last few years dreading the sex within her marriage, as it was loveless and made her feel like a prostitute. Then it was her blooming luck to find someone she wanted to make love to, and now she had found out it would never happen. She said she couldn't be so heartless as to tell me there and then it was over, so she went through the motions of what she knew I wanted to hear. She couldn't bear to upset me. She had realised just how much it had taken for me to disclose what I did to her that day.

The drive back was a surreal one for her and she couldn't even remember the journey. Only her thoughts have stayed with her even now. She wanted to soak in the seriousness of the situation and admitted to even saying out loud in the car, "Can I do this? Forever and ever?"

Integrity is a key element of her character. She would not want to make the decision lightly and then have to revoke it in a few weeks' time. She had to be certain. She mulled it around in her head for the 7-mile drive back to work. She said, by the time she had got into the car park, she was sure she could cope with a sexless relationship. She wiped her eyes and felt positive that she could do forever and ever. As long as we carried on loving each other as we had done, her love for me was enough. It was kind of sad, though, that a physical relationship was not to be.

I had no idea about what she had gone through on that journey back, and it was just as well. I would not have forced her to make a choice; I would have told her not to come back. I'm glad I didn't see her tears.

Karen added the finishing touches to my home. Like most men, I wasn't even aware it was lacking in "touches", but a woman always finds something it needs. Plants were added to the garden, and a lick of paint was applied here and there. I was trapped in a time warp regarding décor, with not enough money and not enough inclination. I struggled with lifting my right arm, anyway. If I raised it above shoulder level, the joint would pop out. It was not only painful when it went back in, but it could take a bit of manoeuvring and rotating of my arm. I walked with what is known as a dropped foot, so I would go over on it, and this was painful on my ankle. My back would still spasm, and I suffered headaches and neck strain, but on the whole, I was having to endure less pain than a few months previous. Karen didn't mind being hands on, and wasn't bad with a paintbrush.

When I thought about my life then and reflected on my past, it made me realise how much improvement there had been to it.

The kids had their moments of upset, but that is an unfortunate result of divorce and happens to most kids in the same boat. They were upset at the marriage split, and the introduction of Karen's kids on the scene caused mixed feelings for all of them. We were now one of those modern blended families of children and stepchildren. Overall, we were doing a decent job of juggling life's experiences. We took the kids on many excursions. Karen and I were both aware that us getting together also meant the kids were having to be together, and it perhaps wouldn't be their choice to do so. We did our utmost to make it work, though.

Our relationship with each other was going from strength to strength, and we needed the kids to accept us as a couple. We were in no hurry and we knew that there was no way we could permanently be together until the court case with the insurance company was over. We ended up forging a relationship with each other and as a complete family of seven, and yet we still had individual lives. Both of us were running our own households, too. Our love for each other was certainly tested many times over, and yet we still felt bound together. I think it is true to say we both thought of each other as a soul mate, even though it wasn't all plain sailing.

Sometimes I thought the easiest solution would be to end the relationship. I got tired very easily, and although the bouts of depression had reduced, I still had the fear that one day Karen would meet a tall, handsome stranger, fall for him and leave me high and dry. I was also worried about the kids and how difficult they found living together. Maybe it would have been just easier to end our relationship. However, when I came to that moment to tell her, I just couldn't bear the thought of my life without her. I gained some kind of inner strength to overcome the insecurities I had over my disabilities, or the sadness that I had of the kids falling out and bickering. I needed her too much, but I felt selfish, as I still didn't believe I had much to offer her.

Life carried on with little change over the following weeks. There was work to attend, kids to get to school, mortgages and bills to pay. Flowers were planted in the garden. Solicitor's statements were submitted for the court case. Children fell out and made up, and Karen and I were still happy to be together. We were spinning the plates and managing to keep them all from falling. Life wasn't bad. More money would have helped, but we settled into a routine.

One Saturday night, we put on our best clothes for an evening on the tiles. We had decided to try a few pubs in Sheffield. Although I liked to have a drink, it didn't bother me when we went out. Karen would have a few, and I was happy to drive. She looked great in her black scooped top and fitted yellow tartan skirt. I know it sounds disgusting, but honestly, she looked really sexy. She had her black tights and stilettos on, lashings of black mascara and her reddish-coloured lip gloss. She had lost weight with all the running about she did, I suppose. She was 34 and looked younger.

We sat in the new wine bar and I looked at her and thought how lucky I was to have found her. She was her usual bubbly self, and the chat flowed between us as usual. She usually drank lager because it wasn't as expensive as wine, but I decided to push the boat out and bought her a couple of glasses of Chardonnay. We discussed many different topics, including some serious ones, such as speculating when it might be that we could get together permanently.

We had a good night and went back nearer home. We decided to take the car back and continue in the local pub at the end of the road. I then could partake myself in my favourite drink, Guinness. There were a few familiar faces in there and we carried on with the evening. I must have had at least four pints. As I hardly drank, this had an immediate effect on me.

It was gone midnight and everyone turned out of the pub for the walk home. We laughed and giggled all the way home. We didn't bother with a coffee and decided we should get straight to bed.

As we went into the bedroom, we grabbed each other in a drunken clinch. Though both of us were in high spirits, the laughs subsided and we began kissing and holding each other in a tight embrace. We kicked off our shoes and fell onto the bed. I stroked Karen's hair away from her face and felt so happy and relaxed with her. She looked into my eyes with her big brown eyes, and I just felt the urge to plant more and more kisses onto her full, soft lips. She responded and started to kiss the corners of my lips whilst cupping my face in her hands. She looked so warm and soft as we lay side by side, embracing and kissing each other. And then something happened. I felt a stirring in my groin. I thought I was imagining it, but then Karen stopped too. Neither of us said anything for a moment and then I carried on kissing her.

Sure enough, something was happening. I could tell by the look on her face she could feel me, too. I think we both thought that if we said anything, it would break the spell and disappear, and neither of us would be sure. We just let natural progression take place. I just wanted it to last as long as possible. The drink had made me relax and feel more confident. I took control of the situation and started to lift up her sweater and gently massaged her breasts. She relaxed completely and helped me take off her sweater whilst we were still kissing each other passionately.

We were soon undressed, and I remember thinking, *Don't let me down now.*

We rolled together as one, and then I made love to her, completely. I had never felt so much elation after making love as I did then.

It seemed all I needed was to feel relaxed with a woman I loved and who loved me, and it all came together naturally. Not forgetting the help of four pints of Guinness, of course. I was King Super Stud. It had only been once in nearly two years, but I was on top of the world. I was Jack the Lad. I was a proper man again. I wanted to rush out and tell everyone, but Karen didn't think that was a good idea. She seemed to take it all so calmly and matter of fact.

She just smiled, knowing it meant a lot more to me than it did to her, and said, "I never doubted you had balls. You just needed to prove it to yourself. Go and make us a coffee now." She turned over and nestled down in the duvet.

I got up to put the kettle on with a grin as big as a Cheshire cat's.

The smile on my face must have lasted for days. I was like a teenager who had lost his virginity. Two days later, I still couldn't believe it. It's a man's thing, isn't it? The thought that I couldn't do it had a profound influence on what I thought of myself as a person and as a man. That night altered my self-image more than anything that had happened before.

I had to tell my cousin Paul, and he probably could have guessed anyway by the daft grin permanently stretched across my face. For once, there were no silly jokes or smutty remarks. I knew he was genuinely pleased for me. It was a mutual sharing of a moment that he knew meant the world to me. Like I said, a man thing. I didn't go into details. I just told him how I'd had a good night and a few drinks and I said the Guinness had done wonders for me.

I was still smiling, of course, and then I repeated, "Wonders," in a drawn-out way with my drawn-out smile, too.

He looked and said, "Naar! Really?"

"Yeah," I said.

"I'm right pleased for you, Dan. Right pleased."

We both had the daft grin, then.

I felt a bit guilty about the disclosure, as I wasn't quite sure what Karen would think about it. Perhaps it was best not to tell her. That proved difficult, as I had always shared things with her, so I decided to come clean.

I tried to drop it out nonchalantly. "Oh, by the way, I told our Paul about… well, you know… How things have improved for me… well, improved for us."

She just raised her eyebrows and said, "Did you have to?"

"Well, I thought I did, yeah. It just came out." I waited with my back turned to her.

She just replied with an insignificantly sounding "Ok."

I turned and looked at her. She just smiled, and we talked about something else.

I couldn't take love-making for granted after that. The first few times sober were somewhat daunting, and it turned out they were for Karen, too. She was aware of not rushing me, and yet she still had to pretend it wasn't a big deal. She was fully aware that any self-consciousness or awkwardness could set me right back. We both pretended to be cool, yet were so aware of taking it too quickly. My problems were probably 60% physical and 40% emotional. But, hey! After a couple of weeks, we nailed it.

Weeks after this, we suddenly realised we were probably putting too much emphasis on what was happening in bed. I felt I had to make up for lost time, but after two or three months, I was being worn to a frazzle.

I was still struggling to get through the week without feeling extremely tired, and as they say, too much of a good thing can actually be bad for you. One night, I had to send her home because I needed the rest. The funny thing is, I think she actually appreciated the break, too. We both thought we'd better go at it like rabbits to prove a point to each other.

It turned out Karen thought she shouldn't turn down any advances I made, and I thought she was so keen I'd better keep it up, so to speak, to make up for lost time.

I felt a definite change in the way I thought about myself.

When the novelty of my rediscovered sex life had worn off, it obviously settled down to something more "normal."

Years later, a song came out by Atomic Kitten with the lyrics, "You can make me whole again". Although Kerry Katona would probably never guess she would have such a profound effect on a person with a pop song (not in a million years, I suppose), the words summed up how I felt about Karen. That's what she did for me. It was something that I know Gill would never have done for me. I needed someone to have faith in me, and Gill lost that a long time before we split up.

My relationship with Karen changed me. I felt more of an equal partner now. Another hurdle had been faced and overcome. There was still lots to aim at. Life still had its ups and downs, but maybe that was inevitable. My life revolved around children, stepchildren, ill health, lack of finances and a girlfriend I sometimes doubted I could keep hold of. Not to mention an ex-wife and an ex-husband on the scene. I suppose it was hardly surprising there were ups and downs.

We did have to work on our relationship, but we were sticking like glue, and I felt that we both felt it was because we had such a strong bond. However, we did feel the strain from time to time. The legal case was proceeding slowly and Karen and I got little time together on our own. Karen's life was quite busy, and the childminder who looked after her children after school was a friend and neighbour. This had taken a big weight off her mind.

Her childminder, Chris, and her husband, Dave, lived a couple of houses down from Karen. It was a nice modern estate on the right side of town. When she visited me, it involved a seven-mile journey. Chris and Dave hadn't got any children of their own and used to take Liz and Tom, Karen's kids, all over to theme parks and on country walks. Karen was so glad that the kids were so cared for whilst she had to work. Then Chris had some bad news to break.

Dave had been diagnosed with cancer, and quite a virulent strain. This meant he needed an immediate operation and therapy, so Chris could no longer look after the children. This really knocked Karen off her stride. She managed to get another childminder close by, but it was strictly business with this one. There were quite a few children at the house, and snacks had to be paid for, with charges for any "seconds" if the kids requested it. There were more charges if Karen was stuck in traffic, and she had to pay extra for every 15 minutes over the time. The kids weren't particularly happy there and Karen was forever clock watching to ensure she didn't incur extra charges. As any working mum knows, this all adds to the guilt and the feeling she was "dumping" the children with a stranger.

She used to get upset but couldn't find a childminder that lived near enough to her, but I think she would have struggled to find anyone as good as Chris to take care of them. I had a solution. Karen should live nearer to me and then I would take her children to school with mine at the school they went to. It would mean Karen committing herself to a move and to me. I wasn't sure if I had asked too much.

She worried about moving her children from their large modern school, as she was aware that they were still unsettled over the breakdown of her marriage. She gave it some thought and then decided to take the plunge. We couldn't live together yet, but she was going to sell her house and move nearer.

Her house sold relatively quickly at the price she wanted, as the area was quite sought after. She chose a property around the corner from me. She was unsure at first because the house she liked had only two bedrooms and it would need an extension, but she had looked around a few and said this particular one had a nice feel about it. The move went smoothly and meant she had some cash left over. She was going to use this to have an extension built to give her the extra bedroom she would need. The kids were enrolled at the nearby small church school and they settled in rather well.

I would take all the kids to school, along with some of the neighbourhood ones. Karen also helped me out financially. Money was still terribly tight, and on more than one occasion, Karen arrived at my home to see me nearly in tears. I would have received a letter from the bank threatening eviction for not paying the mortgage or maybe a large gas bill I wouldn't be able to pay, and she would help with contributions towards the bills. As she no longer paid child minding fees, she could free up more cash to help me out from time to time. It was a good arrangement and meant that not too big a step for the children would be necessary when we could eventually get married and be together. Maybe it's because of our ages, but I don't think it ever crossed our minds that one day we wouldn't probably be married. We didn't even contemplate being common-law partners.

On weekends, we sometimes went out for the day, even if it was just to window shop. I still couldn't walk too far, but we could drive into nearby villages and have the occasional pub lunch. We always found things to chat about. Even though we'd been together a while by then, the relationship still had a freshness to it, especially when we were out of our usual surroundings.

One particular day. I took her to Charlie Freeman's shop in nearby Eckington. Charlie owned a private motorbike shop, and I regularly went to have a look and chat with

Charlie. When we got there, Charlie saw me straight away and came over to talk.

"Got something for you, Dan. Will just suit you now."

I smiled and said, "No, Charlie. I only window shop now."

He assured me I would love what had just come in. A guy was getting divorced and needed finances to pay off his ex. He coaxed us into looking at this big gold bike.

"See, Dan. It's not a sports bike; it's a lovely cruiser. You'd be able to manage this ok. Comfortable position. Smooth to ride."

It did look nice, but as I could only walk a few hundred metres, I didn't hold out much hope that I could manage a big custom Gold Wing. I looked at Karen and said, "It looks comfy, doesn't it?"

She then told me she had never been on a motorbike so she could hardly judge. I hadn't known that, and Charlie then put two fingers to his mouth and whistled out to his mechanic.

"Steve, come and take this lass out for a spin on this."

Karen blushed with embarrassment. "No. It's ok," she said.

Steve came over and said he'd love to take her out. Karen hesitantly got onto the back of the bike behind Steve. She looked so uncomfortable to be there that I had to smile at her.

Off they went. They didn't come back for another 40 minutes. I was beginning to think they had gone off together and abandoned me.

When they finally came back, the first thing I noticed was the marked difference in Karen's posture. She no longer looked stiff and awkward, but relaxed and comfortable. As I got closer to the bike, I could see her smiling like a Cheshire cat. It made me smile just to look at her.

"You liked it then?" I said.

"Yeah. I loved it," she replied. "We are having it."

"We are what?"

"I am buying. We're having it."

We did buy it that day. Or, to be precise, Karen bought it that day with her extension money. Sorry, kids. We did something completely reckless and out of character.

As we drove home in the car, Karen smiled at me and said, "Dan. Have I really just bought a nine-grand motorbike?"

"Erhhh, yeah, you did."

We both just giggled all the way back home.

We never regretted it once. We spent many an hour on the bike at weekends and some pinched hours in the week when we could. It gave us something just for us to enjoy. Riding through the countryside was lovely. We rode everywhere: the Peak District, Castleton, Edale and Chatsworth. Sometimes at weekends, we went into

Lincolnshire and to the seaside, Skeggy and Mablethorpe. We had some lovely times, and it kept us sane during those hard years.

I found it easier to ride than to walk. The controls were all on the correct side for me, as the bike was a Japanese model, not a British one, which would have been more difficult. The only times we had problems were on the odd occasion when we dropped it over. They are huge bikes, and once they drop over, it is a hell of a job to get them back up, but as long as I only rode it on my better days, we were ok.

I was really thankful that Karen made such a lovely gesture, as I am sure it was more for my benefit than hers. But, as it happened, she fell in love with biking too. My sister, brother-in-law and my mother were all horrified when they learnt I had got another bike. Steve, my brother-in-law, gave Karen a stern lecture about buying it.

"If you had seen him in the hospital on death's door, you would not have bought it for him," he said.

Karen took it quite well and said, "Steve. It's in his blood. After going through what he has done, he still is passionate about bikes. Since I bought it, he has been lifted so much. He now has that extra verve. He needed it, Steve. It's what he wants. He's a grown man, and he decides himself what he wants. And Dan, above anyone, knows that you have only one shot at life, and you need to do what makes you happy. You never know if you are always going to have the chance."

It must have been a good answer because Steve conceded and acknowledged Karen with a nod of acceptance. Ironically, years later, Steve and both his sons were to become bikers, having caught the bug themselves.

The motorbike gave us years of pleasure and made our lives happier in the struggling years. Eventually, I did sell the bike in order to buy a sports bike again, and then I went on to have a series of sports bikes before I hung up my leathers. Even then, it wasn't that simple. I later bought another R1 Yamaha sports bike just for last year. I have retired more times than Frank Sinatra, always determined that was it. Yet even now, I am still the proud owner of a sports tourer and two beautiful classic motorbikes. It's definitely in the blood.

It was quite funny the first time we showed the Gold Wing to Karen's mum. Karen's parents had a static caravan on the coast. It was a lovely day, so we decided to ride to the van and show off our new bike. We pulled up at the side of the van and Karen's mum, Dot, was outside. She looked very annoyed to see a motorbike pulling up alongside their van. I think she was about to give us 'what for', but Karen took off her helmet, and I could see Dot's jaw drop.

She shouted to Karen's dad. "Hey, Harry. Come out here! Our Karen's just come on a big whacking motorbike." She was amazed and asked Karen whose it was.

Karen replied, "Mine. I've just bought it."

Dot said. "Have you lost your senses?"

Karen just laughed and said, "Maybe."

I still remember Dot's face now. It was a picture.

Sadly, Dot is no longer with us, but we had some good weekends at the van on our bike. Sometimes we would take the kids. We would have most of the kids in the car, and Karen would drive that, and then I would take one on the pillion with me on the bike. There wasn't enough room in just one car. Because all the kids wanted a go on the bike, we used to have to change halfway. We would pull in at the George Hotel and swap the pillion kid with one from the car and then do the same again on the way back. Four children would then have the opportunity to ride on the back, and then the one left would have to have a ride out while we were there. Happy days.

CHAPTER 13

HOCUS POCUS

Around the time Karen and I met, she paid a visit to a psychic medium. The medium was an elderly lady who lived in the next village, Bolsover. I knew nothing of fortune tellers, psychics, mediums or the like, but later, I would pay her a visit too, which was to have a profound influence on my road to "recovery".

Karen had been booked for her appointment with the medium by a friend at work who had persuaded her to go with her for a sitting. Karen had been left reeling after a visit to the solicitor when she'd been to file for divorce. Her confidence was shattered. She had been trying to lose a little weight, and she had recently returned to work intending to get a mortgage to put a roof over her and her children's heads. Andrew, her husband, had refused to leave the family home, which had put a lot of strain on her. She needed to pick herself up and get into working mum mode. She needed to rebuild the confidence that had been chipped away in the last few years of her marriage, and gain a little faith in herself.

Karen hadn't been to a medium before, and the idea of doing so was a bit daunting for her. However, as she was just going through a divorce, any prompting as to the direction she should take would be appreciated. She was especially worried that her children would be left without their father and wondered if she was doing the right thing in filing for divorce. A friend at work had convinced her there was nothing spooky about the medium and that she would enjoy the experience, so they went together.

The sittings were done separately. The waiting client sat in the living room whilst the medium used her conservatory for the person having the actual reading. Karen's friend had been a few times and had sung the praises of the medium, stating how accurate she had been with the information she had given her.

When it was Karen's turn, she took her seat in the conservatory. The medium put her at relative ease and explained what a medium does. She said that she may just shoot information which may not link to anything at first.

She then began. "Oh dear! Your husband's got another woman, but you know that, don't you?"

Well, she was right there. She then went on to tell her not to worry about the children and that she must do what she knew was the right thing. She told her that her husband would not stop with the woman he was with, but would then have a few more dalliances. All the women would leave him, and he would finish up a lonely man, but there would only be himself to blame. Karen did feel a little happier that what she was doing was the right thing. She really hadn't got a choice with the behaviour she was having to deal with, but it made her feel a little easier. It's not an easy decision for anyone to make and the fact she had been married 16 years made it even harder. So… so much for the past and present. What did the future hold for Karen?

"You are waiting for a tall, dark, handsome man to sweep you off your feet, aren't you?" said the medium.

"Oh, yes, please," Karen said.

"Well, forget that," she said.

The medium told her she had already met the man she was going to marry. This really confused Karen, as she knew there was no one in her life at the time and there was not likely to be. She had enough on her plate to contend with and didn't want any more complications in her life at all. The medium went on to tell her that the man she was going to marry was called Daniel and that he walked with a limp; that he had suffered an accident and had back trouble. She said that he was bald and wore baseball caps, as he was a little self-conscious about it. She also said he wouldn't work again, and he came with three children. To reiterate her meaning, she said, "And I mean, *he* comes with three children. They actually live with him."

Oh my God! Karen thought it couldn't get any worse, but as she felt she hadn't met such a person, she took it in good humour and thought the message wasn't right.

We had, in fact, met on one of the nights out in town, but the most she probably knew about me at the time was that my name was Dan. She hadn't related the description to me at all. Why should she, anyway? There was no attraction to me at that time.

When she walked out of the conservatory, she approached her friend Chris, who was still sitting on the settee.

"Well, so much for the diet," she said. "You might as well hit me with the cream cakes because what's in store for me is not worth all the effort," and she laughed.

I was to visit the same medium months later, and it was certainly a memorable visit.

CHAPTER 14

MEETING MR DOUGLAS

Numerous statements from solicitors were bandied backwards and forwards for many months. My account of what happened had to be taken down in a statement, and the driver's statement also had to be completed. Answers to any queries were raised, and statements were quantified. Medical reports were obtained from doctors and consultants regarding my current physical state and the prognosis for the future. The medical reports were the part that took ages to iron out, which apparently is quite usual in a case where the defendant is an insurance company.

If the accident victim dies, then there's not much, if anything, to pay out. If the victim has an improvement in health, then again, the compensation is reduced accordingly. The ploy of the companies is that if they draw out the case for as long as possible, there's more of a chance that one of these two things could happen. Obviously, it is just a business for them, and the less they pay out, the better. Of course, this is not the case for the poor accident victim. It gradually wears you down.

I attended meetings with solicitors and was prodded and poked by consultants, and sometimes by my own doctors, to give updated statements of my health. Occasionally, this happened with consultants I had never met before because the insurance company wanted an independent, impartial report. Plus, of course, as each appointment was organised, there would be another few weeks to wait. Then clarifications would be needed on the medical terms, followed by the response statement from the insurance company or my solicitor.

It all took a long, long time as months passed between letters and appointments. It was also very degrading for me. I was sick of stripping off and being prodded and scrutinised. I know a few people who went through a similar thing, and in every case, they settled out of court for what they knew was a reduced bottom-line payout, but the whole system wears you down. Physically and mentally, you are at your lowest point, not to mention financially. It is so hard not to give up and succumb to the tempting out-of-court offers. However, I had hit rock bottom already, and they could not account for that.

I dug my heels in, and I wanted to see it through right to the bitter end. The main reason was not financial, which, of course, was a consideration, but I thought the court case would bring me the result of a public announcement in court declaring that it wasn't my fault. I was an innocent party, and the blame didn't lie with me. I wanted to be exonerated. I wanted closure for myself. I thought if it was proven in a court of law, then it would help a lot with being able to forgive myself. Also, Matt's family would know it wasn't my fault, and it would be of some recompense to my kids and for the breakdown of my marriage. I needed that closure, and I was going to go all the way.

It put tremendous pressure on my relationship with Karen. She understood and said she knew what the package was when she met me, but I doubt she knew just how emotionally draining it would be for both of us. She shared my anxieties. We discussed the way forward and all the statements and reports we received. I still expected her to jack it all in at some point. She shared the stress, yet wasn't even included in any of the decisions with anyone. I think that was what she found the most difficult.

Karen was going to be the one who would hopefully share my future, but she had little say in how we were to proceed legally. My solicitor had advised that Karen should not be drawn into the situation. A disabled man with three kids whose wife walked out on him. It conjures a pitiful sight. Especially a man who, because of his injuries, was unlikely at the age of 32 to be able to have any kind of physical relationship with a woman. (This was, of course, the case for many months initially.) It wasn't expected that someone special would come along, but she did. It was advised, therefore, that Karen would stay in the background.

I must admit that when I agreed to that advice, I didn't expect her to remain with me throughout the five years it took to conclude all the legal stuff. I know she found it very frustrating that she didn't have a voice, yet she would be the one who looked after me when I was ill. She would dash to see me in her lunchtime on days I was laid up in bed with painful back spasms, make me a quick sandwich and a cup of tea. She'd be bubbly and cheerful and flapping all over the place. A quick peck on the cheek and "I'll see you later," and she'd be away, facing the traffic to get back to work on time. She was the one who had agreed to accept the future with me, no matter what might be in store physically for me. Yet she wasn't allowed to have an opinion, not a recorded one, at least.

She was my rock, my salvation, the light of my life. Eventually, I began to trust her, and although it took a couple of years, I did start to believe she wasn't going to run out on me. She loved me and gave me the strength to believe in myself again and accept that I was worthy of being loved. I told her what she meant to me then and still do now, but she doesn't have any of it. She always says it was she who was fortunate to find me. After the end of her marriage, she couldn't have hoped to find someone as sweet, selfless and kind.

However, I still believe I got the better deal. Even now, nearly 30 years on, I am thankful for her, of fate that brought us together, of God, maybe? Not too sure on that one. We are still soul mates now, and I know we'll always be together in this world for as long as we are able. In the next world…? Well, who knows? I at least agree to having an open mind on the hereafter these days.

I often think of Matt and his family. Matt had no voice to express his feelings or give his perception of what happened. Legally, he had no responsibilities, as he was not married and had no children. He lived with his parents as he was too young to have a mortgage or household outgoings. Financially, his compensation was nil. His parents were entitled to nothing, and they got nothing. No apology… nothing. Compensation was strictly on a financially calculated level. There was no acknowledgement at all of what happened to Matt. Nothing more to say, really. His family were left in a void, suffering from his loss.

As my legal case progressed, it was time to meet the barrister who would be presenting my case in court, so my solicitor arranged the appointment. When I met him, he wasn't at all what I expected. I thought maybe he'd be a Rumpole of the Bailey look-alike with an office that smelled of beeswax polish. I imagined shelves full of leather-bound books and ribbon-tied papers piled high on a huge antique desk. However, it was nothing like this. I met him in a small office. He was bespectacled, elderly and dressed in brown cords and a casual-looking shirt. The coat rack in the office donned an anorak, not a Crombie. I felt thoroughly disappointed by his whole image before he even uttered a word. I didn't believe for one moment that this man would be my saviour. Disappointed, in fact, is an understatement. I was completely deflated, and my initial feelings were nothing compared to the rubbish that came out of his mouth.

He said he had been looking out of his window and noticed me walking through the car park. "You walk quite well, don't you, Mr Church? Considering what you've been through."

"Oh. Do you think so?" I responded.

"Improving all the time, no doubt," he said.

"Some days are a lot better than others. I push myself through the pain to achieve what I can."

Off to a bad start, I thought, and he made me feel defensive straight away. After all, he did have the hospital notes (from all the consultants).

I could not lift my right arm above my shoulder without the arm falling out of the socket. I was still unable to use my arm properly and struggled to grip much with my fingers. They were still rotated and would always be like that. Even to this day, I do more tasks with my left hand, even though I am naturally right-handed. I always carry my loose change in my left pocket. Shutting my car boot with my left is second nature to me now. The nerves in my right leg are irreparably damaged. I suffered a permanent 'dropped' foot and I walk on the outer edge of the foot, which means I am really heavy on training shoes. My right leg, as well as being shorter than the left now, is also bowed from the knee down. My shoulder is lower than the other one because of the crunching on impact with the road. The scars on both wrists look horrific because they were operated on so many times.

How I looked, however, was a hell of a lot better than how I felt. I was still taking painkillers most days, having terrible spasms in my back a few times a week, and I lived with constant headaches. My knees were still giving me agony some days, and the pain was etched all over my face. I'd aged tremendously, I thought.

However, in all his wisdom, my barrister thought I looked ok… "Improving all the time… Definitely on the mend. Perhaps even able to do some light work maybe…"

I didn't speak to him at first. My lips were pursed. When I did start to talk to him, he would have been a complete fool if he hadn't picked up on the fact I did not appreciate his sharing his perspective of me and my situation. I thoroughly disliked the man. I explained that there were some days in the week when I didn't even have the strength to get out of bed. Each step I took was painful, even then. What kind of job could I hope to find when I couldn't offer any kind of consistency of even attending a complete week?

"Well, I'm afraid the opposition will see what I see. That you don't seem too bad and that your long-term future could possibly be envisaged to include some kind of employment, albeit limited. Maybe sitting on a chair working on a production line. I do think if we're talking compensation, we could not hope to achieve more than the £60,000 that the insurance company is offering. Seems a fair offer to me."

I looked at him with contempt. I could have quite happily cow-tailed him into next week (if I could have made a fist).

One word from me did it. "NO."

I didn't dare say much more, as I knew I would finish getting upset and maybe say something I'd regret later. I left.

Jim, my solicitor, rang the day after and asked me how the meeting went. I told him what had happened, that I wasn't at all impressed with his attitude, and that I didn't have confidence in his ability to do the best for me. Jim tried to talk me round. He told me he had used him a few times, and that he was ok. He also said that changing the barrister at this stage could knock the case back months, even years. I seemed stuck with him.

I talked it over with Karen, and she said what probably most people would say: that he was a professional and must know what he was doing so, therefore, I should be advised by him. She was probably right.

I had many a sleepless night, and weeks passed. My barrister was awaiting my response as to whether I would accept an out-of-court payment of £60,000. It seemed a large sum on the face of it, but having my career end at 32 meant I still had 33 years to support myself and my family before retirement age. I'd still got quite a big mortgage outstanding. Gill would want her money as part of a divorce settlement, plus I had three kids, Karen and her two kids to consider. It wasn't possible to manage. Karen had said she'd carry on working to help support us, but I couldn't let her. It probably still wouldn't be enough anyway. She wasn't on a bad wage, but it would not be enough. Besides, I already felt sufficiently emasculated without her having to take care of me financially, too.

I went to bed, still mulling it all over. I'd already told Karen that if I didn't receive enough compensation to pay our way through the future, then I would not consider marrying her. She had got upset. I was also upset, but she knew there was no moving me. I am stubborn. I would not be a kept man. Karen had a more romantic view than I did. If I loved her, then she thought we could sort anything else out as we went along. I knew, though, that having no income and no finances could not be overcome. It would be too much pressure, and she deserved more. After all, I had already seen Gill turn into a nervous wreck trying to make ends meet, ringing social services, begging for school uniform grants and filling in endless forms for income support. I could not let Karen go through that. *I* could not go through that again.

Karen called me a few choice words: pig-headed, chauvinistic, selfish (I didn't understand the selfish part). She cried, and she stomped a little, too, but I knew what was right. That's why, when I went to bed on one particular night, I'd had enough of the stewing.

It must have been about four in the morning. I sat bolt upright and made a statement. "He's got to go".

"Who's got to go?" Karen asked sleepily.

"The barrister. I'm going to get a new one. I'll choose him myself."

"You do know this could prolong the case?"

"Yep. But there's no other option."

"Ok. If you're sure," she answered quietly.

"I'm sure."

I slept like a baby after that announcement.

Once I'd made the decision (perhaps I do know where selfish came into it), we got on making new plans, legally and domestically. Karen and I had resigned ourselves to a long courtship. We doubted that we would be married in the near future, and we decided we would still be financially independent. We would see each other when we could, and she was going to stop over a couple of nights a week. It couldn't be much longer because social services would be on our case, and my benefits could be stopped. We didn't want that additional stress, and things settled into a routine.

Karen would stop over one night in the week and at the weekend. We missed each other terribly, but we both realised it was the best way forward.

On the legal front, I decided to get myself a new barrister, and I had a good idea of who I wanted. I had come across him as the opposition on a neighbourhood dispute case with a local businessman who locals (myself included) thought was jeopardising the environment with some of his operational policies. The neighbourhood committee's joint evidence was presented, and we were shot down in flames. The businessman walked out laughing.

I remember the barrister entering the courtroom with his gown swirling, long strides, head in the air: such confidence. He was young with a devilish cheeky grin, quite handsome, and he knew it. He wore a brightly coloured bow tie, and it worked for him too. He was *that* confident. Now, this guy looked exactly like a successful barrister, not like an anorak-clad social worker. I wanted that man to represent me. He was also recommended to me by other people who had used him.

I told Jim who I wanted. He said if that's what I wanted, I needed to contact him at Nottingham County Court Chambers and see if he would accept me as a client. However, Jim did warn me that he would come with a high price tag. I was ok with that. I had to stick it out for everything I thought I deserved or go down fighting. My request was accepted. I had got myself a new barrister— the young Mr Douglas.

Mr Douglas turned out to be everything I'd imagined. He was very thorough and certainly kept Jim on his toes with his requests for action. Mr Douglas took everything in his stride and didn't show any concerns over my case at all. He told him within the first few minutes that £60,000 was a rubbish amount, and he wouldn't even consider any amount below double that amount offered.

"They'll offer more," he said. "They always put a low first offer in."

Life carried on for us at home in the same vein as everyone else's, I suppose. Good days, bad days, ill days, iller days; days when all the kids squabbled and then good days at the zoo or seaside. My love for Karen was as strong as ever, and hers was for me, too. I felt it. Anyone who could put up with all the shit my life had thrown at her and still be around must have done it for love. I started to feel more confident and relaxed about the future, and we gave each other strength.

There were still the black days. The down days. I suppose it was depression, but I didn't realise it at the time. Sometimes, these kinds of days followed a really good family day. I thought of Matt. *What would he have been doing if he were alive? Would he be married? Would he have had children?* I was being optimistic about my future, fighting for the compensation that would give me a life with Karen, and yet he had no future.

I knew that legal justice had to be fought for every inch of the way, but is there any spiritual and moral justice? What was the reason? God knows... or does he? The only compensation I had on the bad days was that I knew I had lived through a few years of adjustment after the aftermath of the accident. I knew I would bounce back and feel better about myself and life after a couple of days or so. At least, that was the way most of the time, except on the occasions around the 10th of May — the anniversary of that fated day.

Karen didn't spot it at first and took it personally. For a few days before the 10th of May, I would become really irritable. Nothing pleased me. I wasn't interested in doing anything or going anywhere. I wouldn't shave. I couldn't eat. Life was the pits. I pushed people and loved ones away with my actions. I wanted to be alone. I didn't want to be happy.

I'd arrange for a wreath I could place at his grave. There was nothing on the card because I didn't know what to say. I didn't feel worthy of being acknowledged as a person paying his respects. I didn't want to upset his parents. I didn't want to upset his mum, but I needed to show him I cared. That I still thought of him.

I didn't mind Karen sitting in the car while I paid my respects, but I didn't want her to accompany me to the grave. She seemed to know this and never asked to go. I'd wipe down the headstone and have my private thoughts. These will forever remain private between me and Matt—and God? Maybe God. I don't know.

I'd take a few minutes to reflect, and then I'd go back to the car.

"Ok?" she'd say.

Just a little nod from me confirmed I was ready to go home.

A few days later, I would gradually start to feel a little better. On the anniversary, I was to follow the same ritual for ten years or more. I was always vigilant and looked to ensure no one else was around the cemetery. I would have hated to upset anyone by my presence. The time seemed right for me to stop.

After about ten years, I began to feel wretched, and Karen and Ian said that maybe it was time to stop. It was time to move on and show respect differently. I decided then to visit the grave sporadically, and I would just wipe the headstone clean and ponder a little while. I didn't go at anniversary time again, which made it easier. I do have definite views now as I accept my own fallibility. I would like my headstone to be quite traditional, except for having a red motorbike on it, taking the road to heaven, perhaps (a touch of my spiritual side coming through again). It's a comforting thought for me and always makes me smile when I think about it. It's not at all maudlin.

Mr Douglas familiarised himself with every element of my case in next to no time, and he seemed so blasé about it all. He didn't even look as if he had to work at it. We had a few appointments, and then he asked to see Karen. As she was hardly mentioned in our meetings, I found it a bit of a surprise when she was summoned to his office. She did, too, but I think she was quite pleased to be acknowledged, at least. She donned a nice dress and jacket, applied her makeup and went to the appointment.

When she came back, she relayed to me what had taken place. Mr Douglas had been very open and direct and didn't partake in any banter at all. It was straight to the point. She said the appointment was over very quickly. He asked her where she saw herself in a few years' time, and she'd said happily married to me. He asked what she saw in me (I've asked myself the same question many times). At this, Karen said she gave him one of her looks. She has never been frightened of stating her case and proceeded to do so in this instance. She explained that, for years, she had been married to a very academic, professional man who had achieved quite a high status in his field but made her and her children's lives utterly unbearable. Just when she had thought there was nothing left in her life except being lonely and a single parent, she had met me. She then said what a wonderful man I was, using some more really lovely adjectives. I can't fault her; bless her. She then said she ended with, "If you think I am in this for the money. Then you are mistaken. No amount of money could compensate for all the stress and heartache endured to get through this. I've been with Dan a few years now, and I don't have any plans of running off anywhere."

Go, girl.

Mr Douglas said, "I just had to be sure. I don't want to put everything into this case to find that in a year or so, you decide to break up and move on with half of the money."

He then said he was happy to proceed with the same amount of energy and attention that he had given the case so far. He then gave her a charming smile, shook her hand, and the meeting was over. Karen was left feeling really bemused by the whole thing. She wasn't sure she wanted to kiss him or kick him. I'm sure it would be the former of the two; as I've said, he cut a dashing figure.

There were more statements and appointments, but not many with Mr Douglas. There were some interesting appointments with psychiatrists; I had to see one myself. What a waste of time that was. I didn't even know what it was all about. Karen had to see him, too. He looked a real weirdo. He asked to see her at my house and didn't want me there.

He came to the door, a really portly old gentleman with a long grey beard and a dark blue suit that was well worn and crinkled. He muttered something as he came in, and I showed him into the living room where Karen was seated. I asked him if he wanted a cup of tea, which he declined, and I left to go into the garage to get out of the way.

He stayed for about 30 minutes and then left. I was really bemused by it all.

I then went back into the living room and said, "Well?"

"Like you," she said. "Not really sure what the handle is."

A few months later, I was to learn that there was more to the visit than she first told me, but when she told me, she said it wasn't important. At the time, I think she felt it was a sensitive issue and decided not to tell me. Apparently, he had asked what influence she thought the sexual problems had on my life and how it would affect us as a couple. However, she said he seemed to find the subject very embarrassing. He stuttered and mumbled through his beard, so much so that to help him along, she decided to guess what he was saying and hoped she had guessed his questions correctly. She felt it would be far too difficult for him to repeat them again and didn't want him to feel any more uncomfortable than he was. Talk about 'Physician, heal thyself.' He obviously needed some counselling so he could talk about sex without having to grow a beard to hide behind and relying on his clients to take pity on him. Karen and I were both polite, and we saw the bumbling, mumbling psychiatrist to the door. Poor man, I hope he got help.

He did manage to give Karen some advice. He said it was possible that I was making sperm in my body, and if we wanted children, it might be viable. Then there was talk of consultations and syringes or something. I remember saying to Karen that we had five kids, a mortgage, not enough income and a big court case to face. Did he really think that we would even consider adding a baby to the family?

"As if..." I said loudly with a smile.

I didn't notice her face as she answered quietly, "Yes, as if..."

I should have perhaps registered the wistful look on her face afterwards, but I'm an insensitive man, and I didn't.

When we talked years later about our 'What ifs' in life, she said she had asked me what if we could have more children - would I have wanted a baby? It had never entered my head as being a possibility. The wistful look then registered with me, and I realised then how insensitive I could be.

"I'm sorry," I said quietly.

She just jerked her head back and beamed at me and said, "Oh, don't be. It was only a 'What if?'"

CHAPTER 15

COURT ROOM DRAMA

We were eventually given our dates for court. It was going to be over three consecutive days at Nottingham Crown Court. Five years after the accident, our time had come. I was going to be able to state my case and then get closure. Well, legal closure for this particular battle, at least.

Karen drove us to Nottingham, and we parked in the large multi-story car park. We got out of the car and held each other's hands tightly as we walked towards the court. She looked lovely in a jade-coloured dress with a tiny navy pattern on it and a matching jade jacket and navy shoes. She smiled reassuringly at me. Her hair was bobbing on her shoulders in big brown curls, and her lips were glossed with a lovely, shiny, dark pink coating. Her encouraging smile gave me a burst of encouragement, so my strides lengthened, and I gripped her hand tighter.

We gave our names at reception, and we were told to take a seat. We sat on the hard-backed chairs apprehensively. I looked down at my shoes. I had always had good dress sense. Well, I think I have. My black Oxford shoes shone, and I wore my dark navy trousers. They were years old, but I had invested in them then because they looked so smart, and I brought them out on such occasions. I had on my navy blazer, a plain-coloured shirt and a silk tie (a present) with mustard and maroon swirls. It gave my outfit a lift of colour. I didn't want to look too sombre. Karen had told me I looked good, but I didn't need her to tell me anyway. I felt comfortable and smart. I looked at Karen, and she smiled back. We were ready....

Jim, our solicitor, was there, and it had been decided that Karen wouldn't take the stand. My legal representatives thought it was for the best, but they had said she might have to be called to take the stand. Again, not mincing his words, Mr Douglas said if she did happen to be called, she may have to answer some very sensitive and personal questions. He asked her how she thought she would cope.

She looked at him very seriously, the beam disappearing from her face. "Mr Douglas," she said, "Dan has gone through hell these past few years and physically will probably always suffer pain. I came into his life fully understanding what I had taken on, and we have battled together to get to this point. If you think for one moment that we have come this far not to state our case after all this time, you are very much mistaken. We have been awaiting this day. If you think we may feel embarrassed over a question that may be asked in court, then you really don't understand how much this day means to us."

She got quite choked up, and I looked at her and squeezed her hand a little.

Mr Douglas looked completely unfazed and said, "Good. That's what I wanted to hear." He smiled at us both and then, with his typical confident, perhaps even arrogant air, said, "Don't look so worried, you two. *I* am your barrister. It's in the bag." He then swept down the corridor, his gown flowing behind him, as blasé as you like.

We were then summoned to go in. We were both overawed by the scene. We looked around the vast court. There were lots of people there, including Jim, our solicitor and the representatives from the insurance company who were the defendants. Mr Douglas was down at the front. We could see the back of his wig, and to his side, the insurance company's barrister sat. This time, this one did look just like 'Rumpole of the Bailey' as I remembered the character portrayed in the television series. I never thought the court's setting would be like it is in films, but it looked exactly like that.

The judge was facing the court. He was small and seemed quite old, as he had a wizened face. He had a long, grey, curly wig on that hung down to his shoulders. Some words were uttered, which I couldn't hear, and then everything was silent. The judge had some papers in his hand and we watched with an intense look on our faces.

The judge then spoke, telling the opposition barrister (Rumpole) that he had looked at the case notes. He said that he had viewed Mr Church's x-rays and then asked if the opposition wanted to proceed. We saw Rumpole physically shrink back in his seat before us. Mr Douglas smirked at him, already looking triumphant.

Rumpole stuttered, "We do, Sir."

"Very well. We will proceed," the judge said.

Various statements and reports were read out, including the consultants' diagnoses and prognoses. The statements were from me, my mum, my ex-manager from work, my GP, Uncle Tom Cobley and all, is how it seemed. The atmosphere was anything but relaxed, and I could see on Karen's face how emotionally draining she was finding it. I am sure mine must have been the same.

It went on for hours. I wasn't sure how it was going. It seemed to be made up of a rally of statements, and not much was said about them. It was so disjointed and full of legal jargon. Eventually, the court was adjourned for the day.

We came out of the courtroom, both of us quite nonplussed about the events of the day that had occurred. Good or bad, we had no indication.

Mr Douglas swept out of the courtroom, heading towards us. "Don't look so worried," he said. "It's in the bag. Put the champagne on ice… We have a sympathetic judge." He was so cocky. He then walked very quickly down the corridor, books in his arms and his gown flowing.

We drove home emotionally drained. We talked for a few minutes about why we thought it might be going well or not so well, but we just ended up getting more nervous.

We had talked to the solicitor before the court case and were informed that the "biggy" result would be if it was found that I could not work again. Then, I would have to be awarded for loss of earnings, not just for the years that had passed, but for all the working years I had left before I could draw a pension. That would mean for 30-odd years. Without that decision, the reward would be much less, financially, and for me, or should I say for us, it would be a disaster.

As we lay in bed together that night, I could tell Karen was as tense as I was. She was lying still, but I could tell from her breathing she wasn't asleep. I know it probably wouldn't make her feel better, but I had to tell her again anyway. I had to make it clear.

I spoke softly, but clearly. "If I don't get the loss of earnings for my full working life, I can't marry you."

"I know," she replied just as quietly. She knew why. There was nothing else to say.

I would not see her struggle to keep a husband and five kids for the rest of her life. I wouldn't let her do it. Oh, I know she would have. She was lovely and full of life. I couldn't see her turn into an old woman, worn out through duty. I wouldn't do that to her, and I felt it was my place to provide. She knew how strongly I felt about this, and although I knew she didn't agree, there would be no moving me.

We both spent hours lying awake, waiting for sleep to take us, and eventually, it did.

We awoke for the second day of court, probably feeling more refreshed than we should have, considering what had happened the day before, but we were both enthusiastic. Karen chose some clothes equally as appropriate as the outfit the day before and looked as stunning as usual with her pink glossed lips. I chose the same trousers (the only good pair I had) with a fresh white shirt and a blue and grey striped tie from Next.

We both felt quite satisfied that we looked ok, and we made the 25-mile journey to Nottingham Court again. Mr Douglas had a brief word with us and said he thought it was going well. He said he thought we looked far too worried, especially Karen. He didn't realise just how important this court case was to us as a couple. He had no idea at all.

The second day was easier to follow. The first day, more or less, had been taken up with reading statements. On the second day, the defence was putting forward their evidence to say that I could possibly work again, albeit in a different capacity than what I was used to. The evidence was batted forward and back. Still, nothing was too revealing about what we could expect the outcome to be.

Mr Douglas was as confident as ever and stated our case firmly and clearly. He hardly ever looked at his notes at all—totally different from Rumpole's approach.

Another day was over, and we came out of the courtroom. Mr Douglas asked Karen if she had the champagne on ice yet. She just smiled at him timidly, not at all convinced that his confidence was justified.

We went for lunch in Nottingham city centre and decided to go a little upmarket from our usual choice of restaurant. After all, it wasn't very often we visited a big city, and we needed the support of being in a pleasant, laid-back environment. We chose a chic little wine bar with high chrome bar stools, black matt décor, and lots of shiny mirrors and leather settees. There were low coffee tables with newspapers, which businessmen were perusing whilst others were drinking their espresso coffees and others sipped glasses of white wine. We chose a light bite and coffee and quite enjoyed the afternoon. We didn't discuss much about the court case that day. I suppose we had endured enough of it after two days, and it was nice to relax and have a romantic interlude. They had been few and far between these past couple of months. Afterwards, we had arranged to meet Jim at the court. He wanted to discuss something with us.

Jim was his usual self. He had salt and pepper hair, the back of which was hanging slightly over his shirt collar. He wore a grey suit and looked every inch a solicitor, except for a slight fraying on his well-worn shirt collar. Still, I expect that solicitors go very heavy on shirts. He was kind and gentlemanly, with a timid demeanour about him. We both liked him very much. He asked us both if we were holding up ok, and we said we were. He said he thought we had gone through most of the case, and it would soon be over. He had news for us. The opposition had come through with an increased settlement offer and had to put this to us. The offer had been raised from £60,000 to £120,000 if we agreed now and accepted out of court. Jim didn't give anything away as to how he felt about this.

I thought it was the first indication of how the case must really have been going and was quite surprised, especially considering that the insurance company would have to pay the expenses of the court case so far. Mr Douglas came towards us and asked what I was going to do. I knew this amount would still not cover the expense of the next 30 years, but was it nearing the amount that I could expect to achieve? Mr Douglas shook his head from side to side for some reason and then said directly to me. "Do you want to accept?"

"No, I don't," was my reply.

Mr Douglas walked off smiling

Jim just said, "Well, Dan, it's just as well you didn't accept the barrister I recommended, isn't it?" He looked a little forlorn, but I knew Jim was only doing his best for me.

I explained the last barrister just didn't do it for me, and it was no reflection of Jim's ability. Jim said Mr Douglas was a cocky young devil who had him jumping through hoops these past few months for information, but Jim had to admit; the young Mr Douglas was bloody good.

We went home that evening feeling a lot better than the day before. We had an early night to be as fresh as possible for our last day in court.

I donned my usual trousers and blazer and chose a fresh shirt and tie. Karen looked just as lovely as ever in her office clothes, with just the right amount of feminine touches. Off we went for the final time. All our hopes and dreams were resting on the outcome.

Mr Douglas and Jim were there before us. Mr Douglas was still smiling. He gave Karen a look up and down with a smile on his face. I thought, *He'd better be careful with his glances*. I gave him a look to let him know I had my eye on him.

He then turned towards me and flicked my tie over the top of my blazer shoulder.

"Nice tie," he said. He then asked if Karen helped with my dress choice in the morning.

I was getting a bit annoyed with him now. I might be a small-time ex-mining electrician, but that doesn't mean I cannot be credited with good dress sense or a good choice in women, for that matter.

I just gave him a steely-eyed look and said slowly and deliberately, "No, not at all. I am more than capable of doing that for myself."

Mr Douglas gave a little smile and went on his way. I dare say this man certainly gave my solicitor a run for his money in having to produce all the information he required. It was no wonder that Jim felt a little annoyed with him at times. But still, what price can you put on brilliance, hey?

This day in court was different from the others. The defence evidence was getting more intense. The court was shown a video of me going shopping. I was unaware it was being recorded, but it is apparently common practice to employ private detectives to try to catch you out on film. The good thing for me is I felt I had nothing to hide. We all watched the video on a TV in court. It was quite boring. It was a film of me driving to Morrison's supermarket in my car. There was a minute or so of footage showing a man driving my car. You couldn't really tell who it was at this stage, but obviously, it was me inside; otherwise, they wouldn't have filmed it. The car then pulled into the car park and into a parking bay: riveting stuff.

People in court looked quite bored. Even Mr Douglas found it more interesting to look at his nails and dust them down his gown a little, and then he gave them another brief inspection. His eyes were clearly on anything but the film being shown. The judge gave a heavy sigh, and his shoulders lifted up and down. He was bored, too, I think. Then there was a bit of action: I got out of the car and then went into the supermarket. The video then went to a shot of me coming out of the supermarket, pushing a trolley with a few items in it. Still quite boring. I opened the car boot and loaded the shopping into it. I took the trolley back, got in the car, and drove off. No, it never got any better; it was still boring. The film ended.

Rumpole then got up and started to make his observations on the video. We all listened intently to what he was saying. He was speaking, emphasising words as he went along as he obviously thought this would have an impact.

"Here you see Mr Church in his *denim* jacket, driving his car to do the shopping. In his *denimmmm* jacket," he said again loudly with a lot of emphasis on the last syllable of denim.

He must think hooligans and no do-gooders wear denimmmm. Karen and I had a little smirk at each other.

Rumpole continued. "Mr Church is then able to complete his shopping, open his boot and drive off."

Well, at least Rumpole was watching the film.

"As the court can see, he did this task with apparently no trouble at all, even though we are told he has some difficulty with household tasks. And he did all this in his *denimmm* jacket, not dressed in the attire he has on today."

There goes that dirty word again… denim…

Rumpole made his little speech and then sat down. He looked a real pompous git.

Mr Douglas got to his feet, smiling confidently as ever. "Your honour. What we have seen here is Mr Church doing the shopping, having adapted the way he does this, so it looks like second nature to him. He is wearing his denim jacket, and so what? I don't know about my learnt friend here, but I don't go shopping in a suit either, and in fact, I own a denim jacket." His arm twirled in the air above him as he cast an open smile at Rumpole, almost laughing at him.

"Yes. Yes, Mr Douglas," the judge replied. "We get your point, and may I just suggest that you do not carry on your redirection in what has now become your only too familiar flamboyant style?"

"Sorry, your honour," he said, but he didn't look at all sorry.

Mr Douglas also went on to say that in the film, it could be observed that my limp was noticeable as I walked from the car, plus the way my left leg bowed outwards.

My shoulders weren't level, either. He pointed out that I seemed to put the coin from the shopping trolley into my left pocket, using my left hand. He also explained that I closed the boot using my left hand because I cannot raise my right arm above shoulder level, or it dislocates. He illustrated that I do all these things with my left hand with ease because I have used it continually for the last five years.

Nothing could stop the glee written all over Mr Douglas's face or, indeed, the dropping jaw on Rumpole. Mr Douglas concluded that the film shown was not only boring (I think we all agreed with that point, even the judge) but was also a film that backed my case more than against it. The doleful look on Rumpole seemed to say it all. The judge agreed that it wasn't really evidence to substantiate that I could work full time.

I was eventually summoned to take the stand. I felt very nervous. I walked steadily to the stand; a bible was produced, and I swore the oath. I was asked about my health, about the effects the evidence had on my life and my children's. It was very emotional for me. I was asked why I had requested an interim payment for a car. I explained I could not drive for a few years, but had been coaxed back behind the wheel after finding it necessary to complete the shopping, as I couldn't walk very far. I also told them about my main reason for having a car, which was to take the children for days out during the school holidays. They rarely got any treats, and when all the other children were going on holiday, I wasn't able to afford to take them. But at least with a car, I could take them out for the day or pick them up from friend's houses. I had taken them to zoos and theme parks, and at least I would have happy memories of their childhood I could share with them.

Five years with no money, no hobbies, no holidays, and no decent clothes was a very long spell in a child's life, and I wanted them to enjoy their childhood like other children. I was asked how many days out of the week I was ill. I had always declared that on some days, I didn't feel as bad, and it was on these days that I would go out and do things. This was why people may have got the wrong impression overall about my health, as I was only out when I felt well.

I was asked about my motorbike. This I dreaded, because on the face of it, things didn't look too good. I was able to ride my bike and go out on days out. I explained that my partner had bought the bike, which was a Honda, a Japanese bike. As such, I was able to ride it because the gears are on the other side compared to British bikes. On my good side. I also used only the front brake, again on my good side. Karen had bought it after she had a settlement from the sale of the house she shared with her previous husband. It should have gone towards a bedroom extension for her children in her current property, but as the case seemed to be drawing to an end, she had decided to treat us to a Honda Gold Wing. It was a lovely golden cruiser, and sometimes, when the children were with our ex-spouses at the weekend, we could take a welcome break from all the worries and responsibilities. If I felt up to it, we would take lovely rides out into the countryside.

I was surprised I didn't have to answer more questions about the bike, especially from the opposition, but I didn't. Even the atmosphere in the courtroom had slowly begun to turn. Mr Douglas looked less smug, as if he had already enjoyed the triumph of the battle, and Rumpole looked quite dejected.

My ex-manager was called to the stand and gave a lovely speech about what a valued employee I was and how he was sure I would have been promoted to a manager if not for the accident. It was touching and, I think, very honest.

It was time for the summing up. The judge said there was no question that I was due compensation, but as to how much, that was the question or the "quantum" as they called it. Mr Douglas gave his closing speech and summarised all the key points. Rumpole's face drooped lower and lower. Mr Douglas also said that he felt the medical evidence spoke for itself on the breakages and fractures of bones. My doctors always used to joke about the fact that a trolley was needed to carry the x-rays as there were so many. Mr Douglas then seemed to ask a question that was rhetorical.

"Do I need to expand more on the soft tissue injury that Mr Church incurred?"

There was another flourish of his arms as he sat down and a displeasing glare from the judge again, which Mr Douglas pretended he hadn't noticed.

The judge then said the counsel now had to decide the quantum. Rumpole quoted some precedent on how, according to somebody-or-other's law, the number of years for the variant was 13.

Mr Douglas, who didn't seem to be listening as he was polishing his fingernails on his gown again, got to his feet. "I think you'll find that incorrect," he declared.

He gave the page number and statement of fact that Rumpole needed to refer to in the law book he held. "You'll find that the actual variant of years, according to the table in front of you, if the counsel would care to cast his eyes down, is 17 years."

Rumpole began to dither and stutter and was turning the pages backwards and forwards in the book.

"Would you like help to find it?" Mr Douglas said.

The judge had had enough.

"*Young* Mr Douglas, please behave. I am not going to warn you again."

Mr Douglas apologised. He knew he had pushed his luck with his arrogance now. Rumpole sat a dejected man. Mr Douglas looked very pleased with himself. The judge declared that I would be getting compensation for loss of earnings for all my working life. Seventeen times my last annual income was granted. I had got it....

The judge looked at Karen, giving her an empathetic smile. For one moment, I thought she would break down, but she pulled herself together. We walked out of the court together, holding hands and feeling of pure relief.

CHAPTER 16

CLOSE, BUT NO CIGAR

We should have been onto a 'happy ever after' ending, I suppose, but it didn't quite work out that way. Yes, we were thrilled driving home that day, and we spent the evening phoning our family and friends with the news. They were pleased for us, and we cracked open a bottle of Bollinger that Karen had put in the fridge. She enjoyed it, but I wasn't that struck. I would have preferred a Guinness, but I didn't want to spoil the moment, so I drank the champers anyway.

Unfortunately, the party didn't last. It was my birthday the following day, but the stress levels shot right up the scale again. The doorbell rang, and a man, a stranger, was standing there, and he offered me an envelope. *A birthday card, maybe.* I instinctively held my hand out to take it from him.

"Mr Daniel Church?" he said.

"Yeah, that's me," I replied.

"This is an injunction from the court on behalf of your ex-wife. Consider yourself served with a court order. You are not allowed to touch any of your compensation money until you have financially settled with your ex-wife. Consider the account frozen." He then pulled an apologetic face and said, "I'm sorry."

Happy fucking birthday to you too, mate.

I hadn't even received the money yet, but now I had an injunction that said I could not touch it. It had taken years to fight through the courts for it, and my ex had soon put a stop to my celebrations. It was to be the beginning of a very trying year.

I had been awarded the princely sum of £458,000. A small fortune, or so it seemed. However, after all the deductions, it wasn't anything near as grand. All the years after the accident, I had been receiving various benefits from the social services. These were for income support, school uniform grants, school lunches and the like. All of it had to be paid back out of the award. That took care of over £70,000.

On a couple of occasions, towards the end of the case, I requested interim payments, and I had to put my argument forward as to why I needed the money and how much I needed. The request had to be formally applied for via my solicitor. I requested some money to buy a family car and another payment to help with debts and house maintenance. That came to £10,000, which I had to pay back. I had arrears on the mortgage that I had to bring up to date; another few thousand there. Before long, the sum left was well over £100,000 down.

I never saw all the financial award—not even near that amount—but Gill wanted £100,000 of it. Anger and frustration bubbled inside me. There was no doubt that Gill was entitled to some recompense as a result of the marriage ending. She was legally due her share of the home, even though when she left, she said she didn't want it. For one, she wanted a clean break, but two, when she left, she said she didn't want any part of the bungalow financially. She hadn't paid any maintenance since she moved out, and therefore said she wouldn't claim anything from me for her portion of the family home. However, this was only verbally agreed. She soon changed her mind about all that on the day of the award. Her solicitor was in court to report on how much I received. Maybe the fact it seemed such a large sum of money made her view it differently. Anyway, she wanted a great chunk of it.

Karen was furious. Not at all happy. I simmered and Karen stropped. I understood her point of view. We had suffered years of struggling and emotional turmoil. We hadn't been able to enjoy a courtship in the traditional sense because very rarely had we been on our own. Plus, with my fluctuating health, the continuous stress of fighting the insurance company and bringing up five kids from two families wasn't easy. All this to juggle, and Karen also had to work full time.

The long-term prognosis of my health wasn't great, either. The doctors had told me that my physical health would gradually improve over the first two years, maybe, and then I would spend a few years at a plateau stage. This is where I would have improved as much as I could, and perhaps this would be sustainable for a few years. Then, because of the injuries I had suffered, my health would deteriorate with problems such as arthritis in the joints, back and fingers. Circulatory troubles were probable, which could then have a knock-on effect and compound other issues I might develop. It's not something to dwell on, but there's no doubt old age for me doesn't look too enticing.

The award was to support me and my family as the court had deemed I was unfit for work and the money needed to last me for 33 years until I was old enough to draw my old age pension. I had less than £300,000 left, which, on the face of it, still seems a good sum, but when this is divided by 30-odd years, it calculates out at less than £10,000 a year to live in. Of course, if the amount is invested as a lump sum, then the rewards should be greater than receiving £10,000 a year. The calculation in court was to take this into account, which is why I was awarded 17 years' loss of earnings and not 33, as it was thought that receiving it as one sum would be financially more beneficial.

The ensuing year was a real battle between Gill and me. There were many ups and downs, and unfortunately, I am not proud of myself to say that sometimes the kids suffered and were in the middle. However, I can honestly say that I never used my children as a weapon and did not discuss any of the letters and their contents with them. I never wanted to influence them over what litigation involved between their parents.

I always made it clear to them, or at least I hope I did, that my first wish was to see them happy and not for them to choose between a parent. There were times in the period I looked after my children that I told them if they chose to live with their mum, I would love them just the same. I wanted them to be where they were happiest, and if that was the case, I would see them on days through the week anyway.

We did have a few moments where a couple of my kids thought they might want to live with their mum. I could feel their emotional turmoil when they approached me on the matter. They didn't want to upset me, and they didn't want to upset their mum. I tried to let them make their decisions based on what they felt they wanted to do in their hearts. I didn't pressurise. I told them it was ok if they chose to live at Mum's.

It wasn't until a few years later I learnt from one of them that my quiet acceptance led them to believe I didn't care enough to fight for them to stay. How wrong they were. Like any parent should, I tried my best. Sometimes, I got it wrong, but it was for the right reasons. One child did go to live with Gill, and another cried buckets because they thought that maybe they should. I have had a daughter on my lap, clinging to me and weeping because it was too hard for them to decide. I looked after all my children. My daughter left, but she didn't settle with Gill, and there were tears because she thought she wouldn't be welcomed back. I think she missed the others. Divorce is upsetting for any children involved, and it was just the same for mine.

I wished I could have given them more materialistically speaking. I always felt really guilty that I couldn't give them the things I would have liked. I have, and always will, love all of my children unconditionally and without exception.

I am not a saint, and I know sometimes my emotions spilt over into our family life, but never through insulting Gill or revealing what the latest solicitor's letter was about. Gill felt aggrieved, and I know she told the kids things about me, but I wouldn't retaliate. This doesn't mean I didn't feel like defending myself, but I bit my tongue many times and held back for the sake of the kids' feelings. It was so hard at the time, and I know that sometimes the kids picked up on my true feelings. It seemed so very important then, but now it isn't. I can now just let it wash gently over me without it causing me too much aggravation. It was still raw then. It's true that time heals. The accident, the divorce, and the worry over my children and partner all had an effect on my character and personality. They shaped who I was or who I became. It's life, I suppose.

There was one day in particular that Karen and I laugh about now, but we didn't find it funny at the time. See…? Time heals. It was a Saturday morning, and Karen had decided to do some ironing. She had her bra and pants on and was ironing away. Gill had the children for the weekend. I had my dressing gown on and was having a leisurely breakfast before I got dressed.

To our surprise, Gill's car pulled up on the drive. She wasn't due to drop them off until Sunday. My daughter Rachel jumped out of the car and ran to the door.

She burst into the hall, shouting, "Oh my God, Dad. You can get ready!"

No sooner had she finished than Gill threw open the car door with a face like thunder. I saw what Rachel meant. Something had definitely ruffled her feathers; she was almost breathing fire. She was waving a piece of paper in her hand that was gripped so tightly it was crumpled in her fist. Her partner, Paul, stayed in the car. *Very wise,* I thought.

In the post that morning, she had received the evaluation report on the furniture in my home so that she could claim the value of her half. The independent valuer had been a couple of weeks before and walked around each room with a pencil and pad, scribbling away. At that stage, he had not yet indicated his valuation of the items, but we knew that Gill's request for a few thousand as the value of her half was way off the mark. The report listed broken beds and a telly that had to be warmed up before you could see the picture. A frayed carpet in dusky pink of an 80s swirl design. A settee with a broken leg and saggy upholstery. There were other items of equal quality on the list, no doubt. They came to the grand total of £500. That was £250 to be added to her claim. Gill was livid. She shouted that she had no money and needed some to live on. It was a very strange statement as she was working full time and I was the one with zero income. She then bellowed that I should look for a job and that there must be something I could do to get money for her. I had been used to her volatile nature from the past and decided to ride it out and wait for the melee to die down. Paul must have thought the same as he stayed in the car.

Karen, who was supposed to stay out of any wrangling (advised by our solicitor to keep a low profile), then flew out of the room where she was ironing. She wanted to protect her modesty, so she had put on a non-ironed satin negligee. She had obviously picked it up off the laundry pile that needed ironing. The scrunched satin look and the banshee-looking hairstyle she was sporting (she hadn't combed it yet) added to the overall look. It was like the gunfight at the O.K. Corral.

By this time, Gill's face was a crimson red, and she was still brandishing the letter. Then she threw it at my feet like a discarded gauntlet challenging me to a battle. Alas, I didn't get a chance. Karen, in full battledress, stepped up to the mark. They were nearly eyeball to eyeball.

"Don't you come here with demands for money! If you stopped spending it like water, you wouldn't need to come here asking for more," Karen said. "You should know as well as anyone that he is not able to work."

"Don't you tell me what he is like. I was married to him for 13 years."

"I know that, and you couldn't cut the mustard and sodded off at the first sign of any trouble."

"How dare you stand there in my house telling me anything?"

Oh dear, this was getting too heated. I told Gill to calm down.

She looked daggers at me and said, "Don't tell me; tell her."

I then told Karen to calm down, too. She was none too pleased. There was a period when there was a moment of peace, with both women just eyeballing each other. Doc Holliday, the Earps or the Clantons would not have seemed such formidable characters as the ones facing each other before me, I'm sure. Fingers twitched at their sides as they were thinking about what each other was about to do. Neither of them was backing down. Then, in a flash, Gill quickly turned on her heels and stomped out of the door, much to my relief.

As she got back in the car, she shouted, "Bitch! I'm never going to come on this drive again."

To which Karen shouted back, "Good. At least that's something we can be thankful for!"

Thank goodness it was all over, or at least I thought it was.

But Karen then turned to me and shouted, "This is all your fault. You should have asserted yourself and given her what for. Now look at what you made me do. I have turned into nothing but a common fishwife, screaming on the doorstep for all the neighbours to hear."

She tearfully stomped back through the hall, her loosely belted ivory battledress floating behind her. Her tousled, untidy hair was bobbing up and down on her back. Well, if there is something I have learnt, it is not to interfere with women when their heckles are up.

I retreated to the garage for an hour. That would give her a cooling off time and me a chance to regain strength and courage before attempting to console her. Women are such funny creatures. The best thing a man can know about a woman is to realise that they can never be fathomed and not even to try. I hold my hands up. I don't understand them. In my experience, though, an hour in the garage with a dry cloth and chrome polish or a Haynes manual usually gives her time to sort it all out emotionally.

Relations between Gill and me hit an all-time low and remained that way for a couple of years or more. There was so much bitterness between us. We had moved on from the misery and sadness that the accident had brought to us as individuals and as a couple. Something else more toxic took its place. Perhaps Gill wanted compensation for the years of marriage that she now felt she needed paying for as she had moved on to something different. I wanted to keep the hard-earned financial award, mainly because I felt I more than deserved it. And at least after all the heartache and pain the accident brought, it showed that I won my case in court. I was completely vindicated of all blame and awarded money for compensation as the innocent party. The money said all that to me, and I had very nearly given up the fight on numerous occasions.

Karen had been by my side for most of the painful journey with me. She accepted me for the man I was when I met her, and although I didn't think she would, she stayed with me. I could not provide for the kids and felt much less of a dad because of it. That's not even mentioning the horrific pain I suffered at the time, the ongoing pain I had, and the fact that my health was going to be affected for life. It wasn't a case that she didn't deserve what she was asking for. Maybe in her mind, she felt justified. I know as sure as hell that no money could ever compensate for what I had been through, for what my family had been through.

So, the financial award was far from clear cut. For some, it brought more haggling over a piece of it, and for Karen and me, it wasn't a quick fix to our problems. Yes, it was a great relief to know that the judge awarded the case our way. It was good to know I was believed and exonerated publicly in court. Awarding me the damages from the insurance company meant I was exonerated from causing the accident. It wasn't my fault; it was the car driver's. However, financially, things were very complicated. Gill wanted a big cut. I had to ensure my part was invested wisely so that it would support me into my old age.

On the face of it, Karen and I now had a more financially balanced relationship. However, she always felt she could not allow herself to indulge in things the money bought for being considered some kind of gold digger. She wouldn't allow me to buy her anything, as if she had to prove to everyone she wasn't in it for the money.

People did half joke and say things like, "You've landed on yer feet, haven't yer?"

I know this hurt her as no one knew of all the strength and willpower that had been needed to get through the years up to the court case. On the plus side, however, it did mean we could start thinking of building a future together. No one but us would understand the true implications of the judge's decision. Although the financial award was obviously important, the fact that the judge decided against the driver's insurance company had a much deeper meaning to us than just financial.

It took almost a year of financial wrangling, but within those months were also times of happiness and of "normality". We looked at houses together. I preferred to remain in the same area as the children were at key stages in their education, and I wanted them to stay at the same school. We needed five bedrooms at least as we felt it was important that the kids had their own bedrooms now as they had been so cramped up. We enjoyed house searching like any couple would, but these moments were interspersed with solicitors' letters back and forth, claims and counterclaims.

CHAPTER 17

PEACE AT LAST

Gill was getting more upset as time passed. Money was short, and she needed cash quickly. While we were disputing the amount she should be awarded, none of us could really move on with our lives. There were some fraught conversations on the phone, and it was wearing us all down.

As time passed, the legal fees were mounting for me. As I had been awarded the money, I was no longer entitled to legal aid, which meant I was incurring hefty fees for every letter and counterclaim. In the end, our solicitor said it made more sense financially to settle out of court and compromise with the payment to Gill if we could. Ultimately, the result could mean that I pay for the legal fees and all court costs and might still have to give her a huge chunk, even if we did "win". We had already accumulated solicitors' fees of £13,000, so it made sense just to give her a big chunk. However, I felt that Gill was the one who escaped it all in the early days to move on to pastures new. I was left to battle the case alone whilst struggling with all the problems. I also had been told that my health would deteriorate in my later years and would need more financial support at that time. It just didn't seem fair. Even years after leaving, she could stake such a claim on what was awarded to me.

Karen would have liked to have fought her day in court with her to state our case publicly. She wanted the chance to explain how much we had struggled to get to where we were: how we had tried to provide the kids with as happy a childhood as we could with the limited resources we had. And to prove to the court that Gill didn't deserve as much as she was asking for. Gill even claimed I should pay for the debts that her partner Paul had incurred before he had met her. That was all neatly itemised in one particular letter. I don't know how they managed to put that forward as a fair expense for me to pay.

In the end, I knew the most sensible answer was to settle with her. She had originally asked for £100,000. She agreed to accept £60,000. With the legal fees we had incurred, the amount it cost to pay off my ex-wife was £73,000. We paid it, and we got on with our lives.

We had many a happy day on my motorbike. It's a passion and there is nothing anyone can do about that, even I can't. It's in my blood, and that's the way it is.

I used to keep a framed photograph on my set of drawers in the bedroom. It was my red and black Kawasaki: a lovely bit of machinery. It was beautiful. I know it finished up a mangled mess in the scrap yard, but there was no denying it had been beautiful. Karen had other ideas. She knew motorbiking was a passion for me and had accepted that, but one thing she couldn't accept was the photograph in the bedroom. She thought it was macabre. I didn't understand her way of thinking, but I knew she found it a bit disturbing and put it in a drawer. I still have it and I still look at it from time to time. It was beautiful.

Buying the Gold Wing was a life-changing day for us. We would put our favourite music tape on and cruise down the country roads. I didn't think that I would ever ride again. It was great. We were eventually to get married on that bike, with gold ribbons attached to the front. I wore a suit and Karen wore a little silk Italian number (apparently). The tulip wrap skirt was chosen especially to accommodate her position as a pillion passenger without showing off too much leg. Whatever the fashion terminology was, she looked lovely. She wore a gold hat with a small veil and flowers to accessorise. She had a bouquet of golden orchids—her mum's favourite flower. She was later to place these on her mum's grave. We did wear our white open-faced bell helmets when we needed to.

From those early Gold Wing days, I think Karen began her appreciation of the freedom that biking brings you and the beauty of a warm summer's day and the open road. The bike also came in handy when we were to go on family days out or weekend breaks in Karen's mum's caravan. She would drive the car, and I would take one of the kids on the back. Five kids and two adults were able to get to the coast together.

I kept the bike for a few years. It put me on the road to recovery and gave me back my confidence to think anything was possible. I did part chop it with Karen's approval for a sports bike, a Kawasaki. I carried on gaining confidence and was able to have a few sports bikes after this, including my favourite Yamaha R1 in my favourite colour, red. I no longer have the sports bikes. My injuries took their toll. I know some people can't understand how I could go back to biking after what happened, but it is a big part of my life. However, Karen understood this. She also knew it would be a bike that would put 'life' back into me, and it was. It made me feel like my old self and remember who I was. Who I am. Motorbikes don't cause death, but circumstance and bad driving do. Fate too, maybe.

CHAPTER 18

ANOTHER SPOOKY MOMENT

A few years into our relationship, Chris and her husband had arranged to go to see Mrs Farrow, the medium, again. At the last moment, her husband couldn't go, and as she had booked two places, she asked Karen if she wanted it for me. Karen then asked me to go. No way was I going. *Load of rubbish,* I thought. She said it was only a tenner, and I had nothing to worry about if I didn't think it was serious. She went on and on until, in the end, I said I would if only to prove to her what nonsense it all was. I told her she must have given some clues to Mrs Farrow, or she had gleaned the information from her somehow that she would then use back at you. Making it seem she was giving you titbits of information. Karen said that didn't happen, and I could see for myself.

The house was just a normal-looking semi. Nothing unusual at all. I don't know what I expected, a gothic castle maybe. When it was my turn to 'go through', I was led to the conservatory where two chairs were set out.

"Come this way, Daniel," she said.

I couldn't remember giving her my name.

She then went on to tell me about my aura, which was kind of interesting. Then she told me not to worry about my mum—that she had friends with breast cancer and they were fine. She said Mum would be, too; she would live for many years yet, and breast cancer wouldn't be the thing that killed her. I was gobsmacked. Mum had been recently diagnosed with breast cancer, and I was worried. (She was right, too. Mum died from complications of a stroke years later.)

From that moment, Mrs Farrow had my full attention. She knew about my divorce and meeting someone who was a brunette who would be much better for me. She did say that she knew I was a sceptic, but by the time we finished the session, I would know there was something in what she did. She was right, too.

At the end, she asked if there was anything I wanted to know. Of course, there was, and I wasn't quite sure how to mention it. I must have sounded uncertain. She asked if it was about the accident. Quietly, I said it was. She said she could see Matt, and he was a happy lad standing with his Jack Russell, Spot.

She said Matt told her, "He didn't stand a chance. She came from nowhere." She asked if that meant anything to me.

Of course it did. Matt had said it wasn't my fault.

He asked Mrs Farrow to tell me about the funeral, as I wasn't able to attend. That was true, as I had still been in a coma at the time. He said, "Tell him it was 'blumin' marvellous. Hundreds turned out. All of Brimington. It was really good."

I smiled. Matt would have talked with that kind of boyish enthusiasm. That was all the information I got on the subject, but it meant the world to me. I found some peace that day. I don't think of it as a spiritual moment or the point of any faith-turning eureka moment. It just gave me peace.

I've never been to see another spiritualist since. That one was enough to get what I wanted from it.

I went to see Ian Cummins, Matt's brother. As casually as I could, I told him about the visit to Mrs Farrow. I asked about the dog. I was unaware that Matt had a Jack Russell. Ian said Matt had… well, the family had, but it had died a few years ago. It was called Spot and had followed Matt everywhere.

I went to my garage and opened the drawer where I kept the gloves I had worn on that day. They were useless as the backward force that broke my thumbs had also resulted in the thumb stitching of the gloves being ripped open, so they were badly damaged. I would take them from the drawer and look at them from time to time. A constant reminder of the guilt I felt about Matt being dead and me being alive. If I should dare to forget for a while, then I would look to remind myself.

This particular day, after my visit to Mrs Farrow, I threw the gloves away. I also got rid of the helmet I'd been wearing on the day. I'd kept it, thinking it was the last thing Matt saw before he died. Karen said that was rubbish, as my helmet is the last thing she looks at when riding pillion.

The gloves went, and the helmet, too. It had taken me a few years to realise I didn't need to keep them.

CHAPTER 19

THE PROPOSAL

My marriage proposal was somewhat unusual and unscheduled. The court case was over, but the battle with Gill over the divorce settlement continued. I was still being advised by my solicitor not to get together with Karen yet, as it may influence the case. It had been over four years, and it seemed we were still in limbo.

Karen had some bad news just after the court case. Her mum was ill and had suffered a stroke. She was admitted to hospital, and tests were done. The prognosis worsened each day. The stroke was a result of a brain tumour. Tests were made on the tumour, and it was found to be a very aggressive form of cancer. She was given 18 months to live if she had the radiotherapy treatment and much less if not. Dot was a young 66-year-old, and all the family was gutted. Like any mum, she longed to see her daughter settled in a happier marriage and looked forward to the day when we could be married. Karen's dad, Harry, did everything he could to help Dot. He took her to the Hallamshire Hospital in Sheffield and then to Western Park for treatment. She looked very poorly.

Karen and I went to see her one day. She could talk a little, but the stroke had taken its toll on her state of mind. She tried to speak, but it didn't always make sense. She used to look out of the window and could see the stars in the night sky. But she thought they were angels and fairies and asked us if we could see them and how lovely they were. I looked at her and, out of the blue, told her we had some good news and that Karen and I were getting married in a few weeks. Dot looked elated. Karen looked shocked.

"Lovely," whispered Dot.

Karen still couldn't say anything. I still had the ability to surprise.

When we visited Dot after that, she would talk about how she needed a new suit for the wedding or what she would wear. It definitely gave her a much-needed lift. Unfortunately, she wasn't able to hold out until the wedding and died before the date, but at least she knew. We were glad we got married. We both wanted it anyway. We'd waited long enough, and you can only take so much legal advice. It was the right thing to do for us, too. We carried on with the arrangements and got married a few months later.

We needed the divorce papers—the legal documents to prove we were able to get married. After a search through bureau drawers, we managed to get both sets required for the courts. As a curious recap, we re-read the information on each decree nisi. We were surprised to see that we filed for divorce at about the same time. I had delayed it a little for bonfire celebrations coming up. Gill and I had decided it would best be after that as the kids were looking forward to it so much, so I filed just after the 5th of November. Karen had tried to get her divorce through the courts earlier, in late summer, but in the judge's wisdom, this was delayed as her husband refused to leave their family home. He was refusing to leave his property share.

"Possession is 9/10ths of the law," was his quote on that one. He dug his heels in, or rather his backside, and stuck it out on the sofa, refusing to leave the house. Because of this, the judge thought there was some hope of reconciliation as they were living in the same house. The law is bloody unbelievable at times, but anyway, it seemed that the papers for both our cases passed through the legal administrative system at about the same time. Amazingly, our reference numbers were 9200135 and 9200136, respectively. Our reference numbers were consecutive. We had been lying next to each other in a court office drawer for many months before we even met. What a coincidence that is. Fate maybe… meant to be.

I suppose it is what you call a happy ending, but it wasn't that simple. Many a time, we nearly didn't make it. Many times, I didn't think *I* was going to make it. I look at

Matt's photo in my study from time to time. I have come to terms with the past a bit now. Something happened, but not only to us two on that fateful day on the final journey. The repercussions will reverberate forever within his family. Especially his mum. It's so hard to lose a child. Maybe she will blame me for being that person who drove the bike that day, regardless of not being at fault… technically. I will always carry that guilt with me: that I couldn't save him. However, I have come to terms with the fact that we were in the wrong place at the wrong time, and for whatever reason, I came through it, but Matt did not. I don't think of the 'what ifs' and 'whys' anymore. I just grasp each day.

Karen and I have been married for many years now. Yes, it would have been nice to have our own children together, but we have children and lots of lovely grandchildren. It still makes her smile when I do something off the cuff. When we were struggling for money, I bought expensive bottles of champagne and tins of red salmon, and we sat in the garden enjoying our luxuries. She always made a token protest about it.

"It's cost too much money. We don't have the time."

I have to remind her to live every day as if it's your last and enjoy it.

She smiles and relents. Life is too short not to celebrate it. Life is full of sadness and hardship, but it's also full of love, joy, and happiness. You just have to accept that as being in the now, grasp it and enjoy…

We are well into our 60s, but on a good day, Karen and I put on our motorbike gear, don our helmets and ride off into Derbyshire. The countryside still amazes me—it's some of the best in the country. We sit and have a coffee at the Barrel Inn near Eyam and still hold hands as we look out over the Derbyshire Dales.

Printed in Great Britain
by Amazon

36239547R00142